T0040155

# The **Bonsai** Book

Racehorse Publishing

# Dan Barton
# The **Bonsai** Book

## The Definitive Illustrated Guide

Copyright © Dan Barton, 1989

First Racehorse Publishing edition 2019

First Published by Ebury Press, part of Ebury Publishing, a division of The Random House Group Ltd

All Rights Reserved. No part of this book may be reproduced in any manner without the express written consent of the publisher, except in the case of brief excerpts in critical reviews or articles. All inquiries should be addressed to Racehorse Publishing, 307 West 36th Street, 11th Floor, New York, NY 10018.

Racehorse Publishing books may be purchased in bulk at special discounts for sales promotion, corporate gifts, fund-raising, or educational purposes. Special editions can also be created to specifications. For details, contact the Special Sales Department, Skyhorse Publishing, 307 West 36th Street, 11th Floor, New York, NY 10018 or info@skyhorsepublishing.com.

Racehorse Publishing™ is a pending trademark of Skyhorse Publishing, Inc.®, a Delaware corporation.

Visit our website at www.skyhorsepublishing.com.

10 9 8 7 6 5 4 3

Library of Congress Cataloging-in-Publication Data is available on file.

Cover design by Mona Lin
Designers: David Playne, Miles Playne, and Karen Wilson
Editors: Gill Davies and Alison Goldingham

ISBN: 978-1-63158-379-7
Ebook ISBN: 978-1-63158-380-3

Printed in China

For Cecilia, Julian,
Philippa, Henry and Daniel
with all my love

# Contents

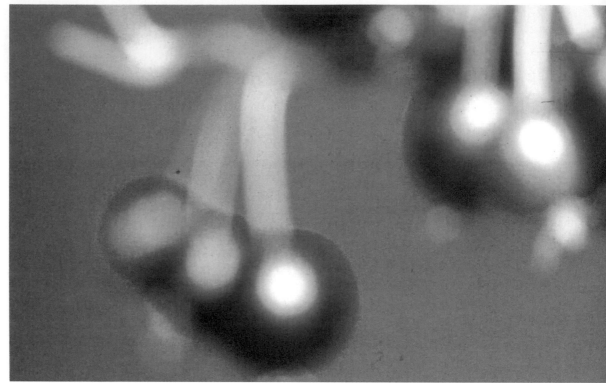

# Preface

The idea of writing a book on Bonsai occurred to me shortly after I became involved with the art in 1969. In those days there were very few books available on the subject in England, so it was difficult for me to find information of any real consequence. I therefore resolved to pursue my own researches and to conduct a number of experiments from which I could gain more practical knowledge about growing trees in miniature. I had no idea at the time what an extensive undertaking this would prove to be, and if I had, I think I would probably never have bothered to continue with the project. I am now very glad that I did, as the direct experience has proved much more valuable to me than anything else that I have done.

All of the practical techniques, hints and tips described in this book are based on my own personal experiences with the subject of Bonsai and on extensive discussion with friends, and can therefore be offered as tested and proven fact. The selection of photographs that I have included to illustrate any salient points are evidence of this.

My original intention in writing the book was to supply usable information based on the extensive records that I have maintained on the various trees in my collection, and to show how each of these trees has progressed individually. I achieved this by making innumerable photo records with written notes on each tree every year. In this way, I hoped to demonstrate that reasonably convincing results could be achieved in a relatively short space of time. I considered that if I could do this successfully, it would encourage others, who might otherwise be put off by the time factor involved, to gain the necessary confidence to make a start. This, therefore, was the basis of my thesis and I hope that the examples I have included in Chapter Seven will illustrate the point. Each of the trees featured here has been subject to one or other of the many techniques or structuring concepts described in the book and the results are well within the capabilities of most people.

Wherever possible I have tried to convey my ideas, whether philosophical or technical, in such a way that they will provoke further thought and not just provide sets of instructions to be obeyed without question. If this were the case, it would contravene any principles I have as an educationalist and mean that I would have failed in my efforts.

It is therefore a pleasure and a privilege for me to share my experiences and any skill I may have acquired with you, and hope that in time you too will gain from these experiences and add some of your own innovative ideas to this most fascinating and fulfilling subject.

Dan Barton.

◀ The author's garden

# Bonsai
## A way of life

*Today
is or was
yesterday's
tomorrow*

Bonsai is for most people essentially a practical hobby and the general consensus of opinion is that it originated in China several centuries ago. However, this practice of growing plants and trees (mostly flowering cherries, pines and chrysanthemums) in pots can hardly be referred to as Bonsai in the way that we know it today. These potted trees were probably used for social or religious ceremonies as well as for decorating the home and were occasionally depicted on ancient Chinese scrolls. They are considered in the context of Bonsai probably because the illustrations suggest that they have been intelligently pruned and positioned within their pots.

► *A typical tree — solid and reassuring*

▼ *Trees come in all shapes and sizes*

Bonsai is about trees; trees grown in miniature. It is also about time and space and about life and attitudes.

At a transcendental level Bonsai can be the intermingling of spirits, of concepts and attitudes, affecting both the trees and the Bonsai enthusiast. Equally, Bonsai can be just another horticultural pastime requiring no more than a measure of common garden sense, some artistic ability and plenty of patience.

Whatever significance Bonsai may have for the individual is open to interpretation. If rules are to be laid down then it is my conjecture that these rules should serve as no more than guidelines or a lot of stereotype trees are likely to result. I sincerely hope that anything written in this book is seen purely as a suggestion or stimulus, hopefully triggering off ideas and associated theories or techniques that the reader may have experienced or, would like to experience.

Art is something that is often expressed intensely, and though it may respect many traditional attitudes and philosophies and be the result of well-established techniques, it nevertheless always offers the artist the opportunity for further experimentation and personal expansion.

Break the rules to make the rules! But first, what are the rules? Dare I commit myself in saying that there aren't any, or at least none that are absolute. Yet this book is crammed full of ideas and techniques and what would appear to be rules. However, this is all that they are; ideas, techniques and disciplines (rule is too strict a term) that I have experienced over many years and which I now offer to you for consideration and possible use. Bonsai and its artistic expression is about mental images responding to aesthetics, which is defined as that branch of philosophy dealing with the nature and perception of the beautiful. The practical

(horticultural) side allows these images to be applied in respect of any given tree and all that can be associated with it: its typical form, the environmental influences that might modify this shape or the abstract ideas that might have a bearing on it.

Of course a tree is a tree is a tree is a tree, whether it be a larch, oak, pine or crab apple. Whatever the species, the environment in which it is growing may have a significant influence on it. It may be formally upright in structure with absolutely straight branches if growing in well protected open parkland. It may have a gently curved trunk making it more informal when growing on gently undulating banks where the wind direction changes regularly. Stronger prevailing winds or landslides may cause trunks to slant slightly or appear windswept. Trees growing under rocky outcrops and cliffs may well reach out for light and ventilation in a semi-cascading manner,

whilst trees growing high up in ravines may duck their heads and cascade downwards to escape the rigours of extreme cold, wind and sandstorms, in search of better climes. These five basic trunk configurations establish the structural order of Bonsai styles and this is covered in more detail in Chapter Three: Styles and styling.

The main point is that Bonsai is an illusionary reflection of nature in its infinite variety, produced under controlled conditions with truth, order and beauty being the prime factors for consideration when styling a tree.

Before moving on to, the origins of Bonsai, let us consider the poem that opened this chapter. Today, yesterday or tomorrow are all relative and their occurence in the eons of time may or may not be of significance. How often one hears a Bonsai enthusiast say, 'Wait till you see this tree next year, it'll be great!' Remember the poem —

next year will have been last year if this year were the year after next. It is all too easy to fall into the trap of allowing Bonsai to become an exercise in wishing one's life away. Bonsai is a way of life, and the joy derived from it should always be for today, and for anyone at any age, whether already involved with it or whether considering the prospect. Planting the seed of a tree in a pot or contemplating the majesty of a mature Bonsai is immaterial; both evoke a sense of joy at any given moment in time. That moment, when it is experienced, will be in the present, and that is, today!

Bonsai by literal translation simply means 'tree in a tray', or in contemporary terms: potted plant. But we couldn't be further from the true spirit of Bonsai if we restricted our interpretation in this way. It is indeed a tree in a pot, but a tree that has been subjected to a number of horticultural and aesthetic disciplines through which visual harmony and botanical well-being is achieved. The essence of classical Bonsai is to produce a healthy miniature representation of a tree. This is achieved by observing nature and noting the salient characteristics that typify any given species and by introducing these characteristics through Bonsai training techniques so as to arrive at a balanced and convincing result. The final statement may be derived from any or several of nature's phenomena. For instance, the overriding influence may be based on trunk status — formal upright, informal upright, slanting, semi-cascade, cascade or perhaps some other facet such as multi-trunk, root-over-rock, split-trunk etc. These qualifying factors determine a Bonsai's style and serve as a useful way to describe a tree which will be discussed further in later chapters. Always remember that although a Bonsai is a tree in a pot, not all potted trees are Bonsai.

Finding the 'soul' of a tree and helping it to manifest itself is a very rewarding experience. Some people talk to their trees and plants; I prefer to listen to mine and after a time (often years), I occasionally hear the message, and that is the moment the Bonsai is

▼ *Bamboo canes*

▲ *Willowherb seed heads*

amongst the most rapidly developing of leisure pastimes in the UK and attracts extensive interest in North and South America, Canada, Australia, Hawaii, South Africa, India and many European countries, so its popularity appears to be growing worldwide.

Although Bonsai is very much a Japanese art-form, its migration to other parts of the world has resulted in many new ideas, philosophies and techniques being adapted to extend its creative scope. These interpretive modifications have been further supported by the addition of new tree species indigenous to the host countries, hitherto unavailable to the Japanese. For example, eucalyptus, ficus, Scots and many other pines; oaks, baobabs, taxodiums, numerous junipers, sequoias and others. Each of these species has its own typical form and current Bonsai trends are in favour of respecting these forms rather than subjecting them to too much distortion. Although, running parallel to this, there does exist another popular facet of Bonsai. This promotes very abstract forms that bear little resemblance to trees as we appreciate them in their natural environments but which nevertheless emerge as satisfying living sculptures and as such are entirely valid. This is most evident in some of the variations of the driftwood style.

So, Bonsai is a continually changing art-form greatly dependent on the aesthetic, creative and technical abilities of the Bonsai enthusiast. It also takes into account the horticultural requirements necessary to maintain each tree within its designed state and the changes that may effect that state for the whole of its life.

conceived and I understand how best to present it. It is at this same moment that tree and man are in total communion, and it does not happen very often. This is Bonsai practised at its highest level: when one transcends the ultimate in practical skills and is then able to reach beyond and enter the spiritual world. A profoundly moving and creative experience.

It is the Japanese who developed the practice into the sophisticated Bonsai that we see, appreciate and perpetuate today. In this form, Bonsai is relatively young,

approximately one hundred to one hundred and fifty years old with a substantial upsurge in interest since the turn of the century both in Japan and the Western world. Unfortunately, many examples of the earlier styles in Bonsai were lost as a result of the Second World War, so it is fairly safe to say that although Bonsai has a long-established history, the aesthetics of contemporary Bonsai is to all intents and purposes less than one hundred years old.

Recent statistics have suggested that Bonsai is

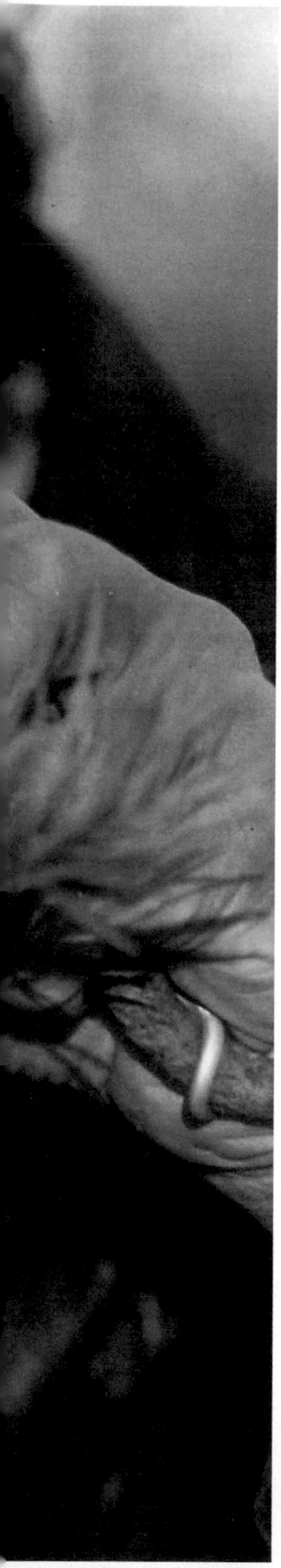

## Making a start

Mirror pool image
silently reclines a toad
Narcissus perceived

## Bonsai sources

There are many sources for material stock. The most obvious is to buy from a Bonsai grower or importer. Alternatively, wildlings or container-grown nursery stock can be used or you can propagate your own tree from seed, cuttings, graftings or layerings. These latter four sources will be covered in detail in Chapter Five.

It is always advisable to seek the advice of an experienced Bonsai enthusiast before making a purchase as Bonsai can be very expensive and, in inexperienced hands, can soon die. If you do not know any Bonsai enthusiasts, then ask at your local information centre or library for details of the nearest Bonsai society. You will find them most helpful.

Each species of tree has a different requirement, and this can be further complicated by the age of the tree which at certain stages will require specific care. It would be unwise for an absolute beginner to start off by purchasing several specimen Bonsai. On the other hand, most dealers offer a wide selection of stock trees or potential Bonsai (Potensai) and these would make ideal introductory material. Larch, pines, mountain maples, cotoneasters, crab apples, spruces, cypresses, birch, hawthorn, zelkova (Japanese grey bark elm), hornbeam and beech are a few varieties that are very hardy and, generally, very forgiving. Within this selection are coniferous, deciduous, flowering and fruiting trees as well as trees that besport spectacular autumn colour.

▶ *Berberis in the autumn.*

▼ *Imported Bonsai Acer palmatum (Kyo hime). An example of a tree that can be purchased from Bonsai dealers.*

▲ Blackthorn (Prunus spinosa) collected from the wild in 1974 and planted on rock in November 1977 — where it has remained to date.

## Wildlings

The next source is from the wild. Without any doubt, the finest examples of Japanese and probably other nations' Bonsai have emanated from collected trees. But the landowner's permission must always be sought before any digging-up takes place. Many a fine Bonsai started its day as a self-sown seedling at the bottom of its owner's garden. So look around your garden and see what it has to offer by way of Potensai (potential Bonsai).

When digging up wildlings of any size for Bonsai training make sure that ample soil around the rootball is lifted with the tree to reduce damage to the roots. Dig a trench

about six to nine inches (15-22cms) radius around the base of the trunk to a depth of ten to twelve inches (25-30cms) and then carefully undercut to sever the tap root and other downward-growing roots. This is usually sufficient to lift most Potensai. Better still, if there is easy access to the tree, treat it as a two-stage exercise. Firstly, dig the trench as described above, then fill it with a

▶ Dig a trench around the base of the tree and remove the rootball very carefully removing as much soil with it as possible. Rootwrap in hessian rather than polythene.

►Prune off any large unwanted roots before planting and stand the Potensai (potential Bonsai) in a vitamin B1 solution for about twelve hours.

▼ Treat the cut with wound sealant and then plant in suitable container.

▲ Collected juniper is tied firmly into a container with sphagnum moss wrapped around the lower trunk to increase humidity. It is then placed in a disused coal bunker adapted for protection against the elements. Polythene sheeting is placed over the top and front in the winter months.

mixture of peat and aquarium-size grit to encourage the formation of fibrous roots. A very slight sprinkling of a rooting hormone powder will also help. The following year dig up the tree and it will have a far better chance of surviving.

The best time to dig wildlings is in early spring when the buds just begin to show signs of awakening from winter dormancy. Or, alternatively, in autumn when the tree begins to enter dormancy. Personally, I prefer the spring, as trees lifted in autumn require protection from frost and the hazards of winter — although this can be overcome by placing them in a cold greenhouse.

Any tree dug up from the wild will have sustained considerable shock to its system. To make the transition easier it would be better not to plant it directly in a Bonsai pot but to nurture it in a large wooden box previously treated with a wood preservative such as Cuprinol. It should remain in this box for a season or two to enable it to recover and develop a strong set of roots. A vitamin B1 compound such as Superthrive or its equivalent can be watered on to the compost of the freshly potted tree. This often helps to alleviate some of the shock and facilitates root initiation. I like to stand any freshly collected Potensai in a solution of Superthrive (diluted in the ratio of ten to fifteen drops of Superthrive to one imperial gallon (3.8 litres) of water) for about twelve hours. This enables the tree to take up a good supply of the vitamins and gives it a far greater chance of surviving — although I have no scientific evidence to support this.

Prior to planting any freshly collected Potensai make sure any large roots that have been cut are treated with a suitable wound sealant obtainable from any garden shop. It is also very important that freshly planted trees are carefully stabilized by tying them down firmly to the container or to a suitable post if they are planted out in a garden nursery bed. Stable trees will regenerate their root systems far sooner if sheltered from movement which is mostly caused by the action of wind. Protect from direct sunlight too.

## Container-grown nursery stock

▶ Typical container-grown stock plant (Pinus sylvestris var. Beuvronensis). Although this is a 'tree in a container' it can hardly be classified as a Bonsai in this untrained state.

▼ Bonsai created from container-grown stock purchased in 1974. See also Chapter Seven: Case histories, for details of this tree.

Garden centres offer one of the best supplies of material stock for training into Bonsai. There is usually a wide variety of species available, and much enjoyment can be derived from visiting different centres. Bonsai enthusiasts are always on the look-out for new nurseries to explore and it is surprising how the adrenalin rises with the sense of expectancy at each new venue. Some of the most unlikely places often have just the right material for Bonsai. This particularly applies to the old-style plant nurseries that still have stock planted out in fields. Here you often find older and sizeable trees that with hard pruning can produce superb Bonsai in a relatively short space of time.

Look out for Potensai that have well-tapered trunks and branches with short internodes and, if the material is grafted, make sure the graft union is as close to the roots as possible.

Look out too for plants that have well-spread root systems, and make sure any trees you buy are vigorous and disease free.

If you are intending to make a forest-group style Bonsai, then choose stock that is closely matched in leaf character and ensure that the trunks are varied in caliper.

Many of my best results were developed from container-grown nursery stock which is one of the quickest ways of creating very convincing Bonsai. You can often apply a good deal of the initial Bonsai training to the tree while it is still in its plastic pot. This is very convenient and often saves a growing season when the tree would otherwise require rehabilitation within a training box.

Another good reason for developing Bonsai from nursery stock is the relatively low cost of the material. One can often buy several plants of the same species so as to experiment with a variety of styles.

Whether you have a predetermined idea of what you want to create, or are just searching for material with potential, it is well worth visiting every garden centre and plant nursery you pass.

## The pot

Containers suitable for Bonsai fall into two main categories: the training container and the display pot. Training containers are used when the tree is in an early stage of development and can be anything from a plastic seed tray to a wooden box treated with a harmless preservative. All sorts of improvisations are possible provided that the container has adequate drainage holes and no undulations in its base to trap water. This is absolutely vital as the major cause of bonsai mortalities is due to root rot resulting from waterlogged pots.

In the early stages it is usual for trees to be planted in over-sized containers. This will encourage better root development which is essential if the tree is to be sustained in a healthy condition.

Display pots are invariably ceramic and, because they must be frost proof, stoneware pots are preferable to earthenware pots. Use only pots that have been glazed on their outer surfaces as roots tend to grip unglazed surfaces better.

Display pots should always be considered and chosen to suit the Bonsai and not the other way round — rather as a picture frame is selected to compliment a picture. The pot, however fine or precious, should always take second place to the tree and should enhance the display rather than dominate it. Apart from the aesthetic considerations, the pot also has an important practical function to perform. It holds the nutrient-rich composts made up from various soil ingredients, fertilizers, air and moisture and also serves as the stablizing foundation for the tree within it. Generally, the pot's length is about two thirds of the height of the tree (if a tall tree), and similarly two thirds of the width if a spreading one. The depth of the pot approximates to the thickness of the trunk just above the root crown. This proportion of pot to tree will usually satisfy both aesthetic as well as horticultural requirements.

Obviously, pots containing cascade-style trees need to be considerably deeper. It won't be necessary to find your ruler; instead, train your eye to discern a balanced relationship between pot and tree. Bonsai by measurement is too

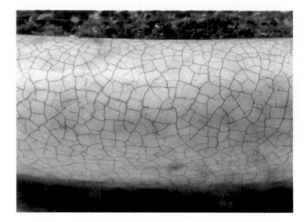

▲ *Glaze crazing.*          ▼ *Glaze drips.*

▼ *Glaze flaw resulting from an air bubble in the clay body. If the flaws are not too extreme they can give individual character to pots.*

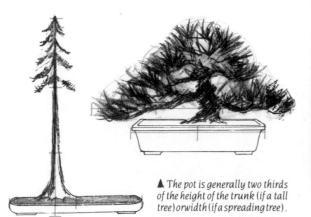

▲ *The pot is generally two thirds of the height of the trunk (if a tall tree) or width (if a spreading tree).*

formulated, and its practice is anathema to any self-respecting artist.

Never be in a hurry to plant the Bonsai in its display pot. Always make sure that the major training regimes are achieved whilst the tree is still in its training container.

Muted colours are generally preferred for display pots whether they are glazed or not, but the 'wee' pots used for 'mame' Bonsai (very small Bonsai never more than six inches 150mm including pot) and for some flowering and fruiting trees can be somewhat brighter and decorated. Conifers are best displayed in unglazed pots bordering on the umber, grey and dull indian red shades. Deciduous varieties on the other hand, often look well in pots that have a subdued glaze and these can be especially pleasing if crazing is evident in the glaze and when variations in the texture and colour of the glaze are also present. Pots that exhibit interesting flaws in their glazes tend to be preferred to pots that are superficially perfect and lacking in character. Avoid pots that look like ovenware.

Choosing the right pot for the tree is a fascinating exercise in its own right, and an harmonious marriage of Bonsai and pot is an image to be savoured.

Bonsai are sometimes planted in or on rocks, slate or stone slabs and glass-fibre fabrications and although these are not pots in the strict sense, they can often show off trees to advantage and portray more natural settings. Once again, visual harmony and functional satisfaction are the criteria on which to base your judgement.

◄ Trident maple (Acer buer-gerianum) due for re-potting.

Before potting up Potensai or Bonsai all excessively long roots should be pruned back and any thick roots dressed with a pruning sealant such as Kyonal, Arbrex or equivalent. Try not to remove soil from the immediate proximity of the trunk base as this will help to form a good rootball. Arrange the roots so that they radiate from the trunk and avoid primary roots that cross over each other. If they cannot be rearranged then prune out the offending roots. Ideally, the root spread should reflect the branch spread of the tree.

Cover the drainage holes in the pot with plastic mesh fixed with copper wires and thread lengths of plastic raffia, string or copper wire through the drainage holes for use as ties to anchor the tree later. To aid drainage, a thin layer of inert chippings should be sprinkled over the entire base of the pot or training box to a depth of a quarter to one inch (5-25mm) according to the size of the pot. Cover this with an appropriate Bonsai compost (see page 28), and then position the tree. (Incidentally, when planting in a display pot it may be necessary to try out several different pots in order to determine the best composition). In the case of trees in training containers, the most sensible position would be slightly off-centre when viewed from either front or side elevations.

Add more compost and work this in with a thin pointed stick such as a chopstick. Make sure the compost is dry as it will fill the cavities around and below the roots more easily. Pull the ties over the rootball in a criss-cross fashion and tie firmly. For cosmetic reasons the top quarter to half inch (5-15mm) of the compost should be covered with a surface dressing such as John Innes No 2 potting mix and to this can be added some dried powdered moss which will start growing after six to eight weeks. This tends to look more pleasing than the stark, coarse potting compost. Never pack down the compost of a newly potted tree as this will compress the minute air spaces between the soil components and reduce the effectiveness of the drainage. On the other hand, avoid any large spaces in the soil which could harbour pests.

Freshly potted trees should be carefully watered in with a watering can fitted with a very fine rose to prevent too much compost being washed out of the pot. Alternatively use a spray for the initial watering, and do not fully saturate the compost until the surface dressing shows signs of drying. Then give the second watering with a can and continue this watering regime for the next few weeks. This will avoid overwatering which tends to clog the spaces in the compost and deny it air, and air is vital in facilitating root initiation.

▲ *Re-pot when buds are just showing signs of awakening from dormancy, usually in early spring.*

► *Remove the tree from the pot and carefully tease out the roots with a bent fork or Bonsai rake.*

▼ *Prune off about one third of the rootball treating any large cuts with wound sealant.*

▼ *Rootball after pruning.*

◀ *Make sure the pot is properly cleaned.*

▶ *Cut pieces of plastic mesh to cover drainage holes and bend pieces of copper wire as illustrated.*

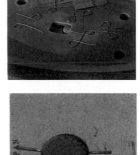

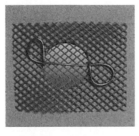

◀ *Mesh held in position with wire seen from above.*

▶ *Mesh seen from below.*

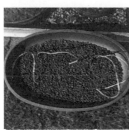

◀ *Thread plastic or wire ties through drainage holes and cover the base of the pot with chippings or Hortag to improve drainage. (This is not necessary when using Mark two compost.)*

▼ *Plant the tree in the pot making sure the dry compost is worked in well with a chopstick. Do not press down as this will compact the soil. Tie in the rootball securely to make sure the freshly potted tree does not rock in the wind as this will damage newly developing roots.*

Refrain from fertilizing freshly potted trees for six to eight weeks as the newly developing roots are very susceptible to chemical scorching. However, it is sensible to add a vitamin B₁ compound such as Superthrive when first watering the re-potted tree, and some people advocate the addition of sequestrated iron such as Sequestrene. This latter product would most certainly be of benefit in the case of azaleas, rhododendrons and ericaceous species.

Bonsai should not be re-potted unnecessarily as the action does cause considerable shock and trauma to the tree. Conversely, root-bound trees are invigorated by the process of re-potting and a change of compost can be of great benefit to the tree. As a general rule of thumb, younger trees in their early stages of training require re-potting more frequently than mature Bonsai that can be left in the same container for up to six years and sometimes more. Again, as a rule of thumb, deciduous species tend to require re-potting more often than coniferous species, and in particular, pines. Exercise caution whenever re-potting, and never re-pot for the sake of it.

One of the main reasons the English need to re-pot more frequently than the Japanese is because of the consistency of the compost. In Britain these tend to be mostly humus based and subsequently break down more rapidly causing compaction, which in turn impedes drainage, whilst the Japanese composts tend to be made up from volcanic-based soils which are structurally more stable and therefore more likely to remain in their original state for longer periods.

▲ *Bird's-eye view of the position of the tree in relation to different pot shapes. Note that the tree is never planted centrally.*

▶ *Water thoroughly with a can fitted with a fine rose and if possible add a vitamin B1 compound such as Superthrive to the water to accelerate root initiation.*

## Composts

The compost in which you choose to grow your Potensai or Bonsai is in effect its sole 'life support' pack, and as such you cannot pay too much attention to its preparation. It should be considered very carefully in terms of the function it has to perform for a particular species of tree at a particular age.

Before going into the specifics of compost preparation there are certain key points to take into account. The compost has physically as well as nutritionally to support the tree; it must be able to drain freely; it needs to contain oxygen in the form of air; it should have the capacity to remain comfortably damp without becoming waterlogged; it should have within its properties a 'buffer' capable of reserving nutrients in a dissolved state; it should be possible to control its pH value; it should not be unsightly in appearance; it should be capable of retaining its physical state for as long as possible to reduce any tendency to compact.

Having said this, there is no single Bonsai 'magic mix', and most Bonsai enthusiasts tend to arrive at their own conclusions concerning the right compost. This, to a great extent, is dependent on the local availability of the necessary ingredients. What is important is that the function of the compost is fully understood and some of the aforementioned points will serve as a useful guide in preparing composts.

Generally I tend to mix a standard basic compost which may then be adapted to satisfy specific requirements. The recipe is as follows:

### Mark one compost

Two parts by volume of Irish moss peat

Two parts by volume of coarse, inert grit (crushed flint, Cornish grit etc)

One part by volume of garden loam (preferably of a clay base)

▼ *Mark one compost before mixing: two parts peat; two parts coarse grit; one part loam.*

▲ *Add some trace element frit to the compost when mixing.*

### Composition

The peat serves as the primary 'buffer' for the retention of moisture. The grit maintains the compost in an open and crumbly friable state, facilitating good drainage and supplying minute spaces for the oxygen requirement. The loam serves as an initial source of nutrients and doubles up as an extra 'buffer'.

Each of these ingredients should be separately sieved and any particles of less than an eighth of an inch (5mm) should be put aside for use in the preparation of composts for mame Bonsai or seed-propagating trays. Any particles over three eighths of an inch (10mm) are too big for the average pot so should be conserved for use in garden beds. Very little need ever be wasted.

To this basic compost add approximately one tablespoonful of trace element frit to every five gallons (22.7l) which will supply all necessary trace elements essential for the well-being of plants. Add also a handful or two of bonemeal which is a slow-release organic fertilizer with a low nitrogen analysis. Further quantities of peat may be added for acid-loving species, and mycelium fungi can be introduced in the form of pine-needle litter from the base of healthy pine trees. This is of special benefit to pines and other coniferous species. (See the section on pines on page 105 for further information.) Leaf mould is sometimes beneficial for deciduous species and so on. You will need to adapt the basic mix to suit the individual trees, so understanding of the specific requirements of each species is essential to making variations. However, for most species I have found the basic mix entirely suitable on its own.

Obviously, the relatively low loam content will

make it necessary to supplement the compost with fertilizers from time to time and this is dealt with in detail in the section on feeding on page 32.

The main drawback to the basic compost mix is that it tends to break down fairly rapidly due to its high humus content. This causes an increase in soil compaction and impairs drainage so that it is wise to re-pot every two to three years. This, as explained in the potting section on page 25, is not entirely ideal, especially for pine species, so I have evolved a more stable compost that is capable of retaining its particle structure for longer periods. The following unlikely compost is the result:

## Mark two compost

One part by volume of coarse inert grit

One part by volume of horticultural pumice (Perlag)

As a growing medium this compost drains excellently; it contains just the right spaces for oxygen-carrying air and the buffering properties of the pumice hold exactly the right amount of moisture with its dissolved nutrients. The compost is entirely loam free and has no other humus-based components except for a quarter of an inch (5mm) layer of John Innes No2 potting compost on the surface purely for cosmetic reasons and as a base to support the growth of moss. Unlikely a growing

medium as this is, I have found that everything that I have planted in it so far is thriving and showing more compact growth with improved leaf colour than has been achieved with other composts. A similar mixture is being used in California with excellent results, and I am undertaking tests to confirm its suitability for use in other countries.

However, it is too early to confirm whether the pumice will retain its structural form over extended periods of time and to be certain of the effects of frost and ice. If it does pass the test of time, it will then prove to be a most important ingredient in the make-up of Bonsai composts.

Provided the particles retain their physical structure this pumice can be recycled and should extend the period of time between re-potting. Its major disadvantage is its appearance, which is off-white and rather bright. It is also somewhat expensive to buy. It is

*▲ Detail of Mark two compost in experimental transparent pot. Note the new roots and the use of a thin layer of John Innes No2 compost or Mark one compost on the surface for cosmetic reasons and to support moss.*

manufactured in Britain by Silvaperl Products Limited in Harrogate, Yorkshire.

Because of the inert nature of this compost and its excellent draining properties, very careful attention will need to be paid to feeding and watering programmes or the Bonsai is likely to starve or dry out very rapidly. On the other hand, overwatering is almost impossible and should you inadvertently overfeed the tree any excess fertilizer can be leached out by running fresh water through the compost.

It is worth conducting your own experiments with composts, taking into account the key points made earlier in order to accommodate local conditions and the indigenous species of tree.

*▼ Rake out the compost and dry it in the sun.*

## Tools

Certain tools are essential to Bonsai training and although it is possible to make do with very few to begin with, as one becomes more involved and adventurous, so the tool requirements increase.

Medium-sized pruning shears and branch side cutters are the first essentials. After this the list will soon expand in the following order of priority: wire cutters; working turntable; various grades of sieve; root rake; jinning tool cum wire-bending tool (see section on the Jin, page 75); jinning chisels and carvers; pruning saw; trunk and branch-bending clamps. You can then build up a range of different sized tools, each with its own special application. Home-made tools can be produced and adapted from other industries; veterinary hoof carvers are ideal for hollowing out trunks, and stainless-steel wire saws (normally used for sawing off the horns of cattle) are very useful for sawing through sappy roots when collecting wildlings.

Many Bonsai enthusiasts are now growing very large trees, so power tools such as chainsaws, reciprocating saws, routers, die grinders adapted for routing, modelmakers' power chisels, power files, angle grinders and so on can all make work easier. Flexible drives with various rasps fitted to electric drills and gas blow lamps are also useful in creating jins (dead branch with bark removed) and sharis (see section on the Shari, page 79). Always make sure someone else is present when working with these tools, in case of accident. Without proper care and attention they can be lethal and should never be abused.

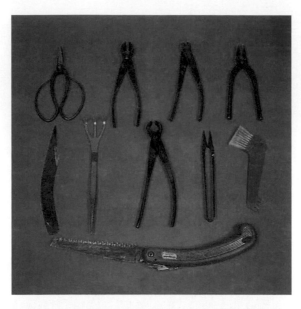

◀ The top line shows the minimum tools required: pruning shears, branch side cutter, wire cutter and jinning-cum-wire bending tool. These can be followed by: pruning knife for tidying up pruning cuts, root rake, wen cutter for knibbling out pruned branch stumps, leaf pruning clippers, brush and saw.

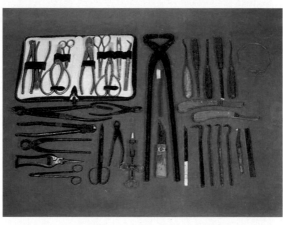

◀ As one gains experience more tools can be added. Top left: boxed set of stainless steel (Masakuni) tools, below which are variations on the basic tool set for beginners, including a syringe which is useful for injecting water into sealed air-layerings. In the centre is a large branch splitter for use with big jins and on the right of the picture is a selection of chisels and jin carvers including, in the centre, two veterinary hoof carvers and top right, a wire saw.

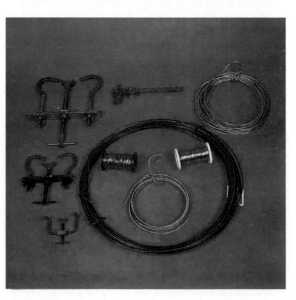

◀ Copper or preferably aluminium wire in different gauges will be necessary and a gauge for measuring the wire caliper is also useful. Branch and trunk bending clamps will help when wire is not strong enough to do the job of bending.

▶ *A selection of power tools useful for Bonsai. Top: Chainsaw for heavy pruning and very large jin initiation. Left centre: model-maker's power set of drills, rasps, wire brushes etc for use in detailing jins (dead branch with bark removed). Bottom left: Power router for carving. Centre: electric drill for general work. Right: Reciprocating saw for cleaning up rough saw cuts made by chainsaw. Flexible lead for use with router and electric drill. Extreme care must always be exercised when using power tools and goggles must be worn.*

▲ *An electric drill fitted with a masonry bit is useful for drilling out planting cavities in tufa etc.*

Obviously a selection of various gauges of wire (preferably aluminium or annealed copper) will be required as well as pruning secateurs, oil stone for tool sharpening, wire and tooth brushes for cleaning bark and refining jins, grafting knives, syringes for watering covered air-layers and all manner of resourceful adaptations.

Building up a comprehensive range of Bonsai tools may take years as the demand increases for more specialized implements. Always take good care of tools and sharpen them frequently as they have so many applications and, if taken good care of, will last for years.

▼ *Bits of broken glass as well as sandpaper can be used to smooth off burrs after jinning.*

▶ *Rasps fitted to flexible leads on electric drills or routers are helpful for carving out dead wood and finishing sharis. Always wear goggles if using a router.*

# Watering

This is possibly the most difficult of all the Bonsai horticultural techniques to master. The watering action initiates a variety of processes, each of which serves a specific need. Unfortunately, most of these processes are invisible and therefore difficult to monitor until the effects of the action become apparent later. This can be shown in the extent of growth in the plant which may be vigorous or weak, and also in the nature of that growth. Is the leaf colour right? Is the needle length correct? Have the twigs become oversappy with excessively long internodes? Why are the branches limp with apparent low turgidity (ie branches that are low on water intake)? Could this be the result of osmosis (a state of chemical imbalance due to overfeeding making it impossible for the plant to take up water)?

There seems to be no end to the actions and reactions that result from the watering process. There really isn't any need to panic about this. Just appreciate that water is the prime means by which nutrients are supplied to the body of the tree and, therefore, the amount of dissolved salts in the water and the quantity of water supplied to the tree will determine the growth and nature of that growth. However, it is important to consider what is required of the watering process.

If an objective can be established then it will be much easier to determine the amount of water required. For example, if a tree such as a mature Bonsai is to be maintained in as unchanged a state as possible, then it needs only enough water (and fertilizer, because these two factors are interactive) to keep it alive. This means a minimal watering programme. On the other hand, if abundant growth and vigour are being encouraged in a young developing tree then

much more water (and fertilizer) will be in order.

Different species of tree may also have different water requirements. Willow and alder, for instance, will need much more watering than pine which prefers to be kept on the dry side.

Bear in mind that watering should not just be a casual activity but one that is designed to satisfy a specific need. Observation and study of each tree and its growth habit coupled with trial

and, hopefully, not too much error, will in time enable the task to be performed accurately and successfully.

Finally, avoid watering in strong sun and in winter water sparingly, especially if there is a chance of the water freezing. Most trees appreciate their leaves being sprayed with water on a regular basis. If it is possible use only rainwater — this will be much better than tap water which often leaves a calcite deposit on the foliage. Water from lime

regions will have an adverse effect on azaleas, rhododendrons and lime-hating species. If this is the case, use water that has been standing in a tub for several days or rain-water.

Always use a watering can or hosepipe fitted with a fine rose to minimize the chance of disturbing the surface compost and, if watering trees that have moss under-plantings, then do make sure the water has penetrated the moss carpet and gone right through to the compost.

# Feeding and fertilizers

Having considered the compost and watering requirements for Bonsai in previous sections, it will now be appreciated that the whole growing environment for Bonsai is quite unnatural. The compost used is rarely more than a growing medium often with a high synthetic make-up and usually containing few, if any, nutrients in its composition. As a result, fertilizers need to be added from time to time to supply all the necessary nutrients to sustain the tree in a healthy condition.

Fertilizers come in all sorts of forms and formulae. They can be organic (made up from animal and vegetable matter), or inorganic (made up from minerals); solid or liquid; for application to the roots or used as a foliar feed. A huge range is available, so where do we begin? Once again, it is a question of being able to define or understand the particular problem and then apply or evolve a suitable technique to effect a successful solution. This may be referred to as one of the design processes and most of the horticultural techniques required for

Bonsai are an exercise in design processes and problem solving. Let's look at one or two examples:

We wish to grow from a seedling a big Bonsai with a heavy trunk and strong branches well bushed out with robust foliage. Solution: feed abundantly with appropriate fertilizer and water well with the tree in a garden bed rather than a pot.

We have a specimen tree which we wish to keep in good health with minimal change to its overall structure. Solution: feed and water very sparingly and only as much as necessary to keep the tree alive and in good health.

We have a flowering tree, a crab apple, for example, which we hope will produce a good crop of fruit. Solution: feed with bonemeal in late autumn then avoid feeding while the tree is flowering or the rudimentary fruits will drop off in favour of vegetative growth; instead, wait until the fruits have set and then feed with an appropriate fertilizer to develop the fruits. This would be a fertilizer low in nitrogen and high in phosphorus and

potassium with a analysis of say, 0-10-10.

We could fill this book with problems and solutions related to fertilizer requirements but by now it must be evident that it is difficult to generalize. Each tree species at any given age has its own special nutritional requirement and this specialized information will need to be gleaned from specialist books on the subject. However, a number of assumptions on fertilizing can be made but first we should examine the analysis and function of fertilizers in general.

The three most common elements essential for plant growth and well-being are nitrogen (N), phosphorus (P) and potassium (K) in their soluble forms. Other necessary elements are calcium, magnesium, sulphur and trace elements such as molybdenum, boron, copper, manganese, iron etc. Trace elements are required only in minute quantities and can be added to composts in fritted form. Frits are very finely powdered man-made silicates with trace elements incorporated

and can be purchased from most large garden centres. It is essential that trace elements are added to both of the composts described on page 28 as they are both virtually soilless.

I tend to use a selection of fertilizers for my trees to make sure all necessary nutrients are provided at some time or other. It is important always to follow the manufacturers' instructions and never exceed the recommended dose. Remember, the roots are in an enclosed environment and if too much fertilizer is given, scorching of the roots will invariably result, particularly with pines and other species that require minimum feeding. Excessive feeding can also set up toxic conditions and result in osmosis when the roots are unable to take up nutrients due to the chemical imbalance in the compost. The tree then dehydrates in spite of any amount of watering. Unfortunately the first symptoms of dehydration begin with leaves turning yellow, then brown, after which they eventually die. When the leaves are in the yellowing stage this often looks like a nutritional deficiency and the tendency is to give more fertilizer. This of course would be fatal. Whatever feeding regime is applied, it is always better to feed weaker fertilizer regularly rather than strong 'dollops' occasionally.

On the whole, organic fertilizers such as fish emulsion, rape-seed cake, bonemeal, well-rotted farmyard manure and even diluted urine — one pound (0.45kg) jam-jar full to one imperial gallon (3.78l) of water — are much gentler in their effect on plants than the stronger inorganic mineral fertilizers. These mineral fertilizers tend to 'burn' any moss that may be used as under-plantings. Most solid fertilizers, whether organic or otherwise, cause slime moulds to form when placed on the compost surface. This can be controlled to some extent by spraying with a fungicide but this may also kill off any beneficial fungi such as mycellium.

## General points to remember when planning a feeding regime:

1 Young developing trees require regular feeding in the growing months with a high nitrogen analysis to promote health and vigour.

2 Deciduous species tend to require more feeding than coniferous species.

3 Azaleas, rhododendrons and other ericaceous species do not like much fertilizing but do benefit from the occasional shot of sequestrated iron and fertilizers that do not release lime into the compost, such as En Mag.

4 Fruiting and flowering varieties prefer fertilizers higher in phosphorus and potassium than nitrogen.

5 Fertilizers with a high nitrogen analysis are good for promoting vegetative growth.

6 Field-grown Potensai respond well to well-rotted horse manure. Growth is the usual requirement so feed abundantly.

7 Foliar feeds and an occasional spraying with magnesiun sulphate (Epsom salts) will improve leaf colour.

8 One year's feeding regime need not necessarily be duplicated the following year. I tend to programme my feeding so that in the first year trees will be fed more abundantly than the following year and so on. This promotes vegetative growth patterns in the first year to capitalize on the benefits of photosynthesis and its effects on root development, and in the second year inhibits growth patterns to check growth and refine twig ramification and leaf size.

9 Never generalize with feeding regimes — try to determine the specific requirements of an individual tree and feed accordingly.

Resist the temptation to try out each and every fertilizer that is available and instead stick with the ones that you know work for your trees.

## Types of fertilizer

A High-concentrate, slow-acting pelleted feed encapsulated in epoxy resin (such as Osmocote) is used somewhat sparingly in the compost when mixed. Its effective life is about four months and it does require warmth to become active.

B General purpose inorganic fertilizer (such as Phostrogen) diluted according to the manufacturer's instructions.

Do not under any circumstances use this fertilizer as a solid feed on the soil surface or root scorching and osmosis are almost certain to result.

C Low nitrogen fertilizer (such as Fisons GH5 or equivalent) for pines and other conifers. This is basically a blood, fish and bone fertilizer.

D Liquid feeds (such as Liquinure, Tormorite or Schultz liquid fertilizer) as an occasional alternative to B above to add variety.

E A 'no lime' release fertilizer (such as En Mag) for rhododendrons, azaleas, heathers etc.

F Bonemeal sprinkled on to every pot as a matter of form in the autumn. It will then be available as a gentle working fertilizer for the awakening roots the following spring.

G Rape-seed cake or fish emulsion are suitable weak feeds for older trees which require containment rather than vigorous growth.

H Root developing and hardening off fertilizers with an analysis of say, 0-10-10 (such as Fisons Fruit Developer No 7 or equivalent) are a useful late-summer to early-autumn feed.

The above fertilizers have been categorized alphabetically to make them easier to refer to when using the Annual Cycles five-year planner in Appendix One. For instance, if a feeding regime is expressed thus: B/D/F, it means that B (general purpose fertilizer) is the main feed with D and F occasional or seasonal alternatives, added probably only once in any growing season.

The analysis of a fertilizer is based on its NPK proportional make-up. For example, 20-8-8 (high nitrogen); 0-10-10 (high phosphorus and potassium), etc. By law, manufacturers of fertilizers are required to indicate the chemical analysis on the pack.

Always refer to the manufacturers' instructions before using fertilizers and keep them away from children and pets.

## Aftercare and situation

When Bonsai or Potensai have been subjected to severe changes of environment or structural status (as with transplanting or extensive pruning etc) they will have sustained considerable shock and will need careful nursing back to a state of health and vigour. Such a shock may occur in the following instances:

1 Collecting from the wild

2 Extensive root pruning

3 Extensive branch pruning

4 Extensive wire training

5 Severe attacks of disease or batterings from the weather

6 Physical damage — eg resulting from breakages due to marauding cats

7 Severe insect or fungal attack

8 Osmosis due to over-fertilizing (see page 32).

9 Extensive preparation of jins and sharis

Most of these conditions can be remedied by making sure the 'patient' is tied firmly into its growing container, watered with a vitamin B₁ compound such as Superthrive, protected from wind and strong sun and provided with an overhead humidity canopy — if possible for about eight to ten weeks. This latter aid can easily be improvised by placing over the tree large wire hoops over which is stretched a suitable clear polythene bag. It is a question of treating the tree rather like a king-sized cutting. The canopy can be dispensed with after the eight to ten-week period but the nursing should continue until the tree shows signs of recovery and stability. In the case of insect and fungal attacks, spray with an appropriate insecticide or fungicide according to the manufacturer's

◀ Improvisations such as corrugated Perspex with a polythene cover makes a good humid environment for convalescing trees.

▼ Cold greenhouses and 'poly' tunnels of any shape or size will be useful for winter protection for half-hardy trees.

instructions and treat as above, but without the canopy.

Not much can be done about physical breakages other than treating the broken area with a wound sealant such as Kyonal or Arbrex.

Trees suffering from the effects of osmosis are much more difficult to treat as diagnosis of the problem is usually made after irreparable damage has occurred. Victims of overfeeding with subsequent osmosis and dehydration should have as much of the residual fertilizer removed from the soil surface as possible; the pot should then be placed in a large container of water so that it is totally immersed. A hosepipe can then be put in the container and water should be allowed to run through it for about forty-eight hours in the hope that all the offending chemicals will be dissolved or leached out.

Make sure that protection from frost and cold winds is always provided to trees

that fall into any of the above categories. Trees that have roots that are susceptible to frost damage (such as Trident maples, yews, Chinese elms, firethorns, oaks etc) and any half-hardy species should be given winter protection in a cold greenhouse, shed or garage. Generally it is the root end of the Bonsai that is most susceptible to frost and ice and precautions should be taken in winter to protect this area in particular. This can be done by placing straw or equivalent insulation material around and over the pot or by burying the whole of the pot in a garden bed. Do not bring Bonsai indoors in winter into rooms with central heating as they will come out of dormancy and produce sappy forced growth with insipid leaf colour and their resistance to disease will be reduced.

Commonsense really is all that is needed in providing suitable aftercare for trees. Just make sure that suspect trees are not subjected to any unnecessary stress.

▼ Bonsai display bench made from two-by-four inch (5 x 10cm) timber in the author's garden. Note that the timber has been stained with ebony coloured Sadolin wood stain and preservative which is a recessive hue so it enhances the display of trees without distracting from them. A lighter colour would tend to predominate. Ample space has been left underneath the shelves for the trees to be placed in winter. Polythene sheeting stretched over top, back and front keeps off frost.

▲ *Paving slabs and flint chippings under display stands. In hot weather the chippings are hosed with water to improve the humidity.*

▶ *This pine is suffering from dehydration as a result of excessive feeding. It has been placed in a large container with running water for forty-eight hours in an effort to leach out the fertilizer.*

## Siting Bonsai

Although it is in order to bring one's prized Bonsai indoors for the odd day or two for display and edification, Bonsai are in the majority of cases outdoor plants and should always be treated as such. They do not appreciate 'molly-coddling' and will suffer, if not die from it.

Ideally, Bonsai should be placed on well-constructed display benches so that when viewed half-way up, the trunk is at eye level.

Not everyone is able to construct or afford a classical display bench but an improvised stand can be built from good quality timber, roofing battens, railway sleepers etc. There are all sorts of alternative materials such as planks placed over concrete blocks or pillars, or concrete sewage pipes or sawn-down telegraph poles; antique chimney stacks with a paving slab placed over the top can make an effective stand for a single tree. The main point to consider is that the stand will need to support valued trees so it must be constructed well.

It would be disastrous if it collapsed under the weight of the trees, or was blown down, or unable to support the extra weight of snow which might settle on it.

Bonsai display stands should be subdued in colour and not detract from the appearance of the trees. If possible they should be sited in front of a plain background to reduce visual 'noise'. The Bonsai should receive a balance of sunshine and shade during the course of a day and should be sited out of the path of draughts and strong winds, although good ventilation is essential. It is a good idea to create a paved area around the base of the stand and place chippings on the ground under the shelves to generate humidity and keep down the weeds. If constructed from timber make sure the wood is treated with a suitable wood preserver or stain such as Cuprinol or Sadolin or their equivalent.

## Recommended species for beginners

Acer varieties; ash; beech varieties; berberis varieties; silver birch; box; cotoneaster varieties but especially (horizontalis); crab-apple varieties; cypresses; elms — European and Oriental varieties; firethorn; ginkgo; hawthorn; hazel; hornbeams — European and Oriental varieties; juniper varieties; larch (possibly the best species for beginners to start off with); myrtles; nandina; pine varieties but especially the Scots pine; pomegranate; potentillas; quinces; serrisas; spiraeas; spruces; stewartia (monodelpha); willows and yews.

Case histories contains specific details and an extended list of trees and shrubs.

There are many more species of tree and shrubs suitable for use in Bonsai but the above list provides species that are generally available (although stewartias are fairly rare) and in most cases easily propagated and ideally suited for the beginner. Included in the list are deciduous, coniferous, flowering and fruiting as well as trees that have good autumn colour. So the selection should cater for most tastes.

There are many other species of tree from which to create Bonsai but initially it would make sense not to be too ambitious as costly mistakes can easily be made.

# Styles and styling

*Spatter, patter rain*
*the patio blotches wet*
*summer day is cooled*

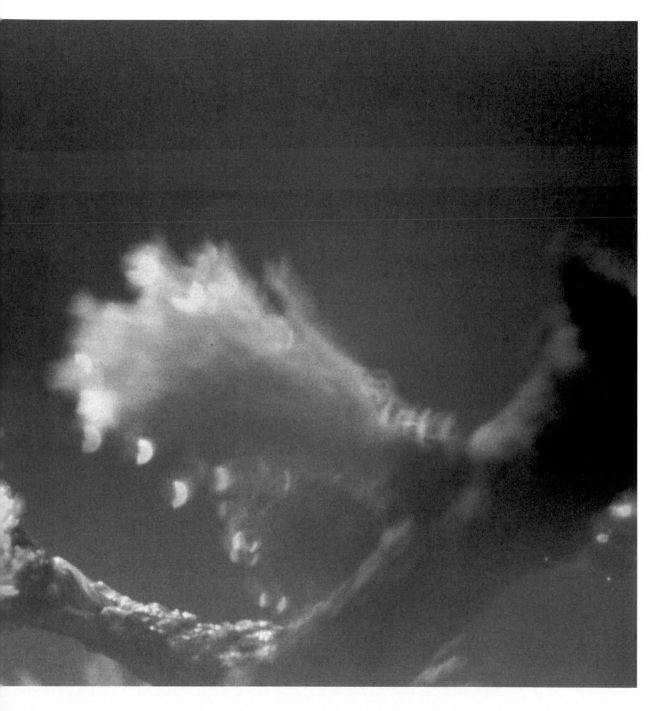

◀ Exaggerated sketch of trees growing in different environments demonstrating the influences of nature in these situations.

To achieve visual balance with inanimate objects is difficult enough at the best of times but with Bonsai we are confronted with a living changing form that alters with time and season, so knowledge and understanding of the horticulture and patterns of growth of any particular species of tree will be necessary in order to arrive at a design solution.

Bonsai styles provide a convenient means of describing tree forms. They vary extensively but mostly emanate from the Prime Order of Five Styles which is the basic structural classification derived from the tree's trunk angle or line. These in turn symbolize natural tree forms that exist as a result of the environment in which they grow. For instance, the formal upright style is a reflection of trees growing in sheltered plains and valleys; the informal upright signifies trees growing over broken and undulating terrain; steeper slopes and windy coastal bluffs produce the slanting style; whilst rocky crags and overhanging cliffs inspire the semi-cascade and cascade styles.

Most other Bonsai styles are variations of the above five but give emphasis to certain attractive natural features and phenomena. For example, root-over-rock style; forest-group style; broom style; driftwood style; split-trunk style; exposed-root style etc. These, and most other styles, all have their origins in nature. Bonsai recognizes these natural curiosities and attempts to present them in an organized and improved manner, often exaggerating certain aspects for visual effect and to generate focal attention.

Styles in Bonsai should serve to inspire the Bonsai designer in his or her expression of tree forms and should not become the accepted formulae. Use the basic styles as a guideline and devise your own way of interpreting them, for although we are concerned with the representation of trees in miniature we are equally concerned with the aesthetics of the tree and its status as an expression within the realms of art — and this gives us an opportunity for innovation and creative thinking.

◀ A schema of the intellectual and practical processes involved in Bonsai design from the author's notebook.

Begin with an idea and search for a suitable material tree    OR

concepts, Ideas and Visual Editing

Continual process of evaluation, editing and correcting to maintain Bonsai in desired style.

seeing tree triggers off series of ideas

Applied Bonsai practice

Aesthetic and Horticultural concepts and techniques

POTENSAI

BONSAI

# The Prime Order of Five Styles

## 1 Formal upright style *Chokkan* and derivatives

The formal upright style is probably the most difficult of all styles to create. This is because the rigid geometry involved in forming the style produces a series of essentially straight lines and overlapping triangles. This means any defects are easily spotted and may result in a compromise tree.

To produce a classical, formal upright style involves a considerable search for suitable material, as branch intervals not only have to be suitably spaced to give gradually diminishing intervals, but also have to be correctly arranged around the axis of the trunk when viewed from above. This may be one reason why it is qualified as formal. Unless you are lucky enough to find such

▼ *Formal upright style larch from nursery stock, trained since 1977.*

material, it is probably best to start off from seed or cuttings in order to control all of the growing stages. Make sure several seeds are germinated to increase the chance of success and select a species that grows fairly quickly, such as larch, or one of the pines, or some other coniferous variety such as yew or cryptomeria (which is easily propagated from cuttings). Air-layering is also a good way of starting off formal upright style Bonsai. Although it is possible to grow some deciduous species in the formal upright style, this remains the exception rather than the rule.

The trunk of the formal upright style must be absolutely straight and have a well-defined taper to it. The trunk should be well developed with a radial distribution of roots that form a sound buttress at the base. The branches should be straight and firm with the largest emanating from the lower trunk and alternating from side to side and slightly forward with a solid rear branch approximately one third of the way up the back of the trunk to give depth to the Bonsai. It is because of this back branch and the important role it plays in providing depth and reinforcing the three-dimensional concept, that we have a front to the tree, or a preferred viewing side. Of course there are other back branches progressing up the trunk.

The overall effect should be a tree that is 'masculine' in structure with no weak points in it and tending towards the

► Upright style (Sequoia-dendron giganteum) from nursery stock, trained since 1977, height 36 inches (93cm).

austere in character. It is an utterly contrived form and rarely looks natural which makes it an uncompromising distinction from any other Bonsai style. For me, the formal upright represents the most elevated state into which a tree can be developed using the art of Bonsai, and remains my preferred style. Without doubt it is the most challenging of styles to create.

It should have a stature and formal discipline that makes it the very essence of the art and when presented at its best, should make the statement: 'I am a perfect tree!' It is the beginning and the end of the art and requires experience and understanding of the many other Bonsai styles before its 'soul' can be fully appreciated. It is the interruption and punctuation of space using a controlled pattern of horizontal elements intersecting a vertical axis to produce a combination of overlapping triangles.

There are also a number of trees which are grown in an upright manner but which do not obey the strict rules of the formal upright style. These trees are usually softer in appearance and look much more natural and are often referred to quaintly as 'tree, trees'. In other words they look more like the trees we see in our parks. The trunk/ branch configurations are simple and light and in no way display the perverse manifestations of botanical arthritis seen in so many Bonsai.

The upright style lends itself to most deciduous species as well as some of the conifers such as sequoia, spruce and varieties that have a tendency to upright growth. It is interesting to note that Japanese Bonsai rarely depict conical forms. This appears to be more of an occidental innovation in tree design.

The points already made about spread of roots and shape of trunk still apply and although the branching is inclined to be more natural in the upright style, it should nevertheless be well structured in terms of space and form. Faults such as crossed branches, bar branches, spokewheel branches etc should be avoided. Branches should feather outwards towards the tree's periphery, progressively reducing in caliper and then gently inclining upwards in the fashion of most parkland trees.

Formal upright style Bonsai should be planted in pots with simple lines and no decoration, in muted neutral colours and almost always rectangular in shape. Upright styles on the other hand, usually look best in pots with slightly softer lines — often oval and sometimes even circular in shape. Again, undecorated pots and pots with unfussy glazes are more appropriate.

## 2 Informal upright style *moyogi*

◀ *Informal upright style Japanese mountain maple from imported Japanese nursery stock, trained since 1974, height 19 inches (49cm).*

The informal upright style is undoubtedly the most accommodating of the traditional styles and also the most popular to contrive, and as a consequence results in more clichéd Bonsai than any other style. It can be used to make a 'silk purse' out of any 'sow's ear' so it is an excellent starting point for Bonsai enthusiasts with minimum experience. Very convincing tree images can be achieved in a relatively short space of time and to minimize the chances of boring repetition one can introduce 'character' by asking a few questions before style training begins. For instance, is our Potensai young or aged; is it lively or staid; attractive or grotesque; chubby or lean; is it cantankerous or austere; tall or squat; elegant or dishevelled? Find the tree's 'soul' before commencing work. This is particularly important if you want to build up the tree's best qualities and avoid producing a stereotype Bonsai.

The major prerequisite of the informal upright style is that the trunk is well buttressed with a good spread of radial roots and that it has a good taper from base to apex. The trunk should sport a series of curves culminating in a crown that is inclined towards the viewing side. This is essential with this style as it reinforces the illusion of depth. Unlike the formal upright style, its lines are generally soft and natural in appearance and it is visually far less static. Although the final statement should be a balanced harmony it must be 'alive' and full in its syncopated rhythms. This can be achieved by selective branch pruning and carefully considered wire training to relate the residual branches to the trunk.

In the case of deciduous species remember the variations in mass that will occur as a result of the seasonal changes with subsequent leaf drop, and anticipate this in your design. Ideally deciduous trees should look attractive in all seasons but this is not always possible. Zelkova elms are a typical example — they generally look far better in their winter state than in the summer state when their leaves can be disproportionately large for the branches and refined twigs.

Visual 'weight' can be established and altered by giving emphasis to a specific part of the tree. Focal attention can be directed to almost any point by applying certain aesthetic criteria. For instance, should a *jin* be introduced (see page 75); what about a large low branch; would a *shari* (see page 79) enhance the image? By eliminating some options you can then concentrate on the right course of action.

Informal upright Bonsai look well in a variety of pots which can be either circular, oval, rectangular or square — depending on the particular tree. The pot should be soft and yet straightforward with minimal to no decoration unless it is intended for flowering or fruiting species. Glazed pots can enhance this style provided the glaze is not garish. The traditional practice is to place the tree in an off-central position — as always you are aiming to achieve visual balance and harmony.

The essence of the informal upright style is to create a series of linear curves in the trunk and branch configurations which serve as structural supports for a 'sky of foliage clouds'.

## 3 Slanting style *shakan* and derivative Windswept style *fukinagashi*

This is a very satisfying style to accomplish but is, for some unknown reason, among the less common of Bonsai styles. This may be because its name, slanting, implies a state of instability, and Bonsai enthusiasts may be put off by this. There is no doubt that aesthetically to balance an inclining form which defies the laws of gravity is no easy task. Unless careful attention is paid to the tree-to-ground relationship it will invariably look as if the tree is falling over. To compensate for this you need to provide a visual counterbalance which can be achieved by building up a supporting buttress of roots or compost to imply an equal and opposite force or by establishing a branch on the opposite side of the incline.

Virtually all visual images are made up from a combination of all or any of the following elements: vertical, horizontal, diagonal and curved. In the case of the *shakan* we are concentrating on the diagonal. It is a force that is usually very unstable in the visual sense and often disturbing to look at. Hence the yellow and black diagonal lines which are so often used graphically to warn of danger. Yet the diagonal is dynamic, and when successfully applied to the slanting style in Bonsai can be superb. The degree of incline will determine the amount of visual 'weight'; the further from the vertical the greater the weight. You will need to establish the Bonsai's centre of gravity, as this will represent the fulcrum from which to steady the swing of the trunk.

Before resorting to pruning and wiring it can be useful to experiment first with plasticine and pipe cleaners to make a mock-up potential tree. Another technique is to photograph the Potensai and then trace the main structure of the tree using tracing paper. You can then draw in any modifications and judge their effectiveness before styling the Potensai accordingly, using normal training techniques. In this way errors in your design can be kept to a minimum.

With the slanting style the trunk may be curved or straight depending on the particular tree, but the roots should play a fairly prominent role and positively 'grip' the soil in a manner which emphasizes support and anchorage of the tree in its curious position.

A favourite variation on the slanting style is the **windswept** *fukinagashi* style which reflects those coastline and clifftop trees we so often see bowing bravely to the winds in their fight for survival. These trees are almost always bereft of branches on the windward side and frequently display large sections of trunk that have been stripped of bark, usually caused by the combined action of wind and ice. They are referred to in Bonsai jargon as sharis.

Windswept style Bonsai are often very contorted and display a powerful visual energy and dynamism rarely seen in other styles. Again, we usually end up with a lop-sided tree with almost all of the branches on one side of the trunk making it a nightmare to balance visually. This can be overcome by keeping the foliage 'clouds' down to a minimum and by arranging them in positions where the trunk provides shelter and confirms their credibility. Windswept styles can often benefit from being grown in conjunction with rock to reiterate the cragginess of their natural environment.

As well as shallow, circular and oval pots, slate slabs, tufa rock and ceramic crescent pots are best for displaying the slanting and windswept styles of Bonsai.

The nature of the slanting style and its derivatives lies in the creation of a Bonsai in which equilibrium is achieved between the visual tension that is set up by the swinging action of the inclined trunk, and the formal organization applied to the tree's roots, trunk, branches, foliage and placement in the pot to counter that force and maintain the tree in a state of visual balance without any loss of the dynamic tension evoked in the tree by these forces. Now take a breath!

▼ *Windswept variation of slanting style larch from nursery stock, trained since 1977, length 27 inches (69cm).*

## 4 Semi-cascade *han-kengai* and 5 cascade *kengai* styles

The semi-cascade and cascade styles differ from the previous three styles within the Prime Order of Five Styles in that their trunk lines encourage downward rather than upward growth. The semi-cascade is exactly as its name implies in that its flow tends toward a gentle curving downward arc, whereas the cascade tree is much more certain in its downward growth.

Rules have been written stating that if the growing tip of the tree falls below the rim of the pot it constitutes a cascade style, whereas a semi-cascade's growing tip would always be above this point. To my mind, rules of such an absolute nature are in no way helpful. The important thing to remember is that the style exists purely to serve as a guideline. If one feels a tree's dynamics are definitely downward in its flow then it would be sensible to describe it as a cascade style. If it is not upward growing but tending towards an outward and gentle downward flow (but not straight down), then refer to it as a semi-cascade.

Both styles are full of life and movement and if the semi-cascade's form can be likened to the graceful curtsy of a lady, then the cascade is more like a plunging waterfall

▲ *Semi-cascade style hornbeam on rock collected from the wild as a tiny sapling and trained since 1972, length 26 inches (67cm).*

bouncing down over boulders and splashing foliage clouds this way and that way. It is an exciting style with many directional changes in its trunk and branch lines.

Both cascade and semi-cascade Bonsai require deeper than average pots in order to achieve a visual as well as physical balance. They are also very suitable for growing on tall pieces of tufa or rock.

The semi-cascade and cascade styles complete the sequence which makes up the Prime Order of Five Styles. However, there are a whole range of styles which may well fall into one or other of the above categories by way of trunk line but which also have their own distinguishing characteristics that give them individual status. A brief description of some of the more popular of these styles follows.

► *Cascade style hawthorn collected from the wild. This was number six in my collection of Bonsai and as such is currently the oldest in my possession. It has been trained since 1969 when it was a tiny seedling. Height 31 inches (79cm).*

# Single trunk variations

## Broom style *hokidachi*

There are several variations of the broom style but in every case the trunk is straight with well-spread roots. In some instances it may divide into two upper trunks which in turn divide into two more (known as major branches), which in turn divide again — so there is a mathematical progression of: one, two, four, eight, sixteen etc. Each of these divisions reduces in caliper until a fine tracery of twigs remains. Alternatively there may be a single trunk line with a series of upwardly inclined branches emanating from it. Another variation is to have several branches around the trunk at approximately the same height, and so on.

The style when seen as a silhouette may be tall, rounded, spreading or squat and is usually structured in a highly symmetrical manner. It is a reflection of the tree forms most commonly seen in parks and lining streets and is best suited to deciduous trees, particularly the zelkova. Beech, hornbeam, stewartia *monodelpha* and Chinese

elms are other favoured species for growing in this style.

Simplicity in form is the essence of this tree and as such it is amongst the most sophisticated of Bonsai styles and like the formal upright style is amongst the most difficult

▲ *Broom style zelkova from a cutting made in 1971. It is one of three that I have felt is worth keeping out of a total of two hundred started in this style. Height 20 inches (51cm).*

to create in its classical state. I am still trying to produce a perfect broom after having initiated well over two hundred zelkovas in this style.

Because of its simplicity in form it is often thought of as being visually boring and consequently is not as popular as perhaps it deserves to be. However, I feel that the broom style represents one of the most pure of tree forms and a profound understanding of it will come only from a mature understanding of the art of Bonsai. If the formal upright style is the purest state into which a conifer can be trained, then the broom style is its equivalent for deciduous species.

Broom style Bonsai are always grown in shallow pots which can be circular, square, hexagonal, oval or rectangular and can often have scalloped corners.

The illustrated sequence on air-layering in Chapter Five explains how broom style zelkova and other suitable species can be created by this method of propagation.

## Literati style *bunjingi*

◄ *Variations in the style of literati. Note the tortuous nature of the curves and the linear quality of the trunks. A very lively style; full of movement.*

The literati style of Bonsai is said to have been inspired by early Chinese scroll drawings of trees on mountains. These highly impressionistic drawings had a certain poetic lyricism about them and were often quite abstract in image. Yet if we look at the European Scots pines, there is a striking similarity to these scroll drawings so maybe the origins of this style are not as contrived as we are led to believe.

In essence the style is highly linear and less demanding in that there should be a significant taper in the trunk. Its meanderings can vary from an almost straight line to the most tortuous of bends, and I tend to liken the style to a 'leisurely stroll into the clouds'.

Because it is so linear in form the spaces circumscribed by the trunk in its progression from roots to apex are vital to the overall design and these spaces should be firmly encompassed by the trunk. Therefore when designing curved literati Bonsai try to introduce bends into the trunk of ninety degrees or more (often doubling back on themselves), rather than using loose swan-neck curves that are visually weak. Of course straight line literati are also entirely valid.

One of the most common faults with the literati style is that the foliage clouds are often far too heavy in their visual mass for the visual weight of the trunk; radical leaf pruning or needle removal may be necessary to redress the balance. Always understate the balance of foliage.

Although the literati style is usually associated with coniferous species and in particular with pines and junipers; some deciduous

▲ *Literati style Scots pine in the upright variation that I collected from a peat bog in 1978. Height 37 inches (94cm).*

species can be used for this style. Cotoneaster horizontalis is a good choice and, in America, buttonwoods are often used. Hawthorns,

flowering cherries, firethorns, Lonicera nititda, nandina, azaleas, tamarisks and even willows can be considered for this style, but it is best realized when coniferous species are used.

The literati style is about as different to the formal upright and broom styles

as chalk is to cheese, but together, these three styles complete my choice of favourite Bonsai forms.

Literati Bonsai are mostly grown in shallow circular pots with convex sides. This is to grip the compost and prevent the rootball from toppling out of the pot.

## Root-over-rock style *sekijoju*

The style in this form of Bonsai is related to its root formation. That is, although the trunk and branch configurations may favour one of the Prime Order or one of its derivatives, the roots and their arrangement over a suitable piece of rock give the Bonsai its individual character.

These roots when mature will combine with the rock to produce an overall form of interesting if not grotesque appearance. Again, this reflects one of nature's phenomena.

To create this style it is best to use young stock of species that develop good root systems (such as trident maple, spruce, birch, yew, pine, Chinese elms etc). Grow the Potensai in a deep container for a season to produce long roots, then in early spring remove it from the pot and wash most of its soil away to expose the roots. Untangle the roots and then place the tree in a suitable position on the rock with its roots spread over it. Choose a well-fissured rock with interesting character and arrange the separated roots down these fissures. The rock should first have been prepared with wire ties strategically positioned and stuck in place with a suitable glue or cement compound. Special cement compounds have been prepared by the Japanese for this purpose and most Bonsai dealers stock them.

Strap the roots down to the rock with these wire ties and re-pot the tree in a deep plastic bag pot until the whole of the rock and root system is covered. Then water and feed well for the next two to three growing seasons to encourage the roots to take a firm hold on the rock. The plastic pot can be cut away in a gradual spiral over the next three to four years allowing the surface compost to slowly

▲ *Root-over-rock style spruce made from nursery stock. This unusual and sophisticated hemisphere of foliage has taken over eight years of continual finger pinching to achieve the symmetry. In training since 1972; height 18 inches (45cm).*

become exposed and to erode away, uncovering the roots over the rock. When sufficient roots and rock have been exposed, the tree can be removed from the bag pot and re-potted in a shallow Bonsai pot. At this stage

remove any wire ties that visually offend.

Another way to train trees in this style is to plant the wire-tied tree and rock directly into a garden bed. This will promote far more vigorous growth causing the roots to swell and consolidate themselves onto the rock much sooner.

Whatever technique one uses, the whole process is very time-consuming in the formative years but if well executed can be most rewarding. The important factor is to select a beautiful piece of rock and one that is unlikely to break down from exposure to frost in later years. The trunk and branches can be trained in respect of any of the recognized styles. The longer one takes in the early stages of training root-over-rock, the more convincing the roots are likely to be.

A variation on this style is **Rock-grown Bonsai**

*ishitsuki* in which the root systems are grown in hollowed-out cavities in the rock containing compost — as opposed to growing over the rock and down into the pot below.

This concept suits single and multi-trunk Bonsai and can be particularly effective with forest groups. Pots are usually shallow in order to give prominence to the rock. They tend to be fairly informal and are often glazed. Occasionally a

▲ *Variations on the style of root-over-rock and rock grown when the roots grow in soil in cavities on the rock instead of over the rock. The style lends itself to single or multiple plantings and the scale relationships between trees and rock can suggest all sorts of perspectives.*

Bonsai grown in the *ishitsuki* style may be placed in a *suiban* (shallow container with no drainage hole) tray with water in it.

## Driftwood style *sharimiki*

To create this style much of the bark needs to be removed from the trunk and branches causing a high percentage of the tree to be rendered dead. The denuded branches and trunk areas are treated, when dry, with a bleaching agent such as lime sulphur (this also has preserving properties) to produce an effect that is very like the driftwood washed up on beaches.

The technique is best applied to older trees as

younger ones can soon callous over cancelling the effect. When handled with skill and sensitivity dead branches (jins) and portions of trunk without bark (sharis) can add considerably to the illusion of age and general mystique of the tree. The style is most commonly practised on junipers but can be applied to most coniferous species and occasionally to some deciduous species.

Hostile environments

create natural victims but to produce a specimen artificially you need to strip the bark off parts of the front side of the tree. It would be pointless removing bark from the hidden side of the tree as the whole idea is to create a visible enhancement that reinforces the total image.

Never remove bark from the trunk below soil level or the sapwood is likely to rot away — eventually killing the tree.

Most driftwood style Bonsai look well in rugged pots that compliment their austere appearance. Informal ceramic crescent pots and large slate and stone slabs can also set off this style well.

When stripping off bark, make sure sufficient is left to continue the lifeline to the living parts of the tree and apply the technique only to trees that are fit and that really will benefit visually from the exercise. On larger trees power

►Driftwood style blackthorn collected from the wild as a rather
leggy sapling three times the
present height. I finally decided to
chop the tree back and jin out the
top branches. After a couple of
years I created the shari and
jinned one or two more branches.
Height approximately 12 inches
(30cm).

tools such as routers and
drills fitted with rasps may
be useful to facilitate
carving of the exposed
areas and a jeweller's
blowlamp can be used to
burn off the hairy burrs.
When preparing *jins* it is
preferable to tear back the
wood with *jinning* pliers
rather than sharpening the
branch to a 'pencil' point.
Torn and broken *jins* look
more natural.

## Split-trunk style *sabimiki*

Some of the classified
styles are really nothing
more than techniques that
have been applied to a
tree to create a specific
effect. This is much the
case with split-trunk style
Bonsai where the trunk of
the tree (which could be
an informal upright,
slanting, driftwood,
semi-cascade style etc), is
literally split longitudinally
down its trunk and prized
apart to create two
elements. It is not a style
that is seen often as it
requires rather drastic
techniques and if the first
attempt does not succeed
there is no second chance

◄ Split-trunk style larch from
nursery stock, trained since 1977,
height 19 inches (48cm).

— the Potensai will usually be ruined. On the other hand, it is a style worth considering as it can be very powerful and dramatic.

This style is best suited to trees with thickish trunks and Potensai that cannot easily be transformed into any of the other classic styles. You will need a large branch-splitting tool to crack open the trunk or a sharp axe which can be used as a broad chisel to cut through the trunk with the aid of a hammer. Once the split is made, wooden wedges can be forced into the crack to open it up and when it has been prized apart sufficiently, a large pebble placed in the crack will hold it open until it finally 'sets' in its split position. This may take up to two years or more.

Because of the drastic nature of the technique the split-trunk style is not to be recommended for beginners.

The preceding styles represent the most popular single-trunk variations of Bonsai and although other styles also exist, they are currently less fashionable (probably because of their rather grotesque and artificial appearance) so they are dealt with here in less detail.

## Twisted-trunk style *nejikan*

This is exactly as its name suggests. It can be achieved in young trees by twisting the trunk along the longitudinal axis or in older trees by peeling off a 'spiral' of bark along the length of the trunk to suggest a twist.

◄ *Twisted-trunk style. Often a strip of bark is peeled off in a spiral to suggest a twist. This can also be achieved by tightly wrapping several pieces of thick wire round the trunk for a year or two until it bites deeply into the bark; this is then removed with the underlying bark to form a twist with the remaining bark. There is a variety of pomegranate that has a trunk that twists naturally.*

## Exposed-root style *neagari*

With each re-potting the tree is raised to expose more and more of the root system until the overall image appears rather like a mythical monster with the roots resembling a tangle of legs. This style can also be created by removing the rock from root-over-rock style Bonsai to reveal stilt-like roots — a rather esoteric style in Bonsai design. In nature one sometimes sees this phenomenon on trees growing on river banks where the river has eroded so much soil from beneath the roots that they become quite exposed.

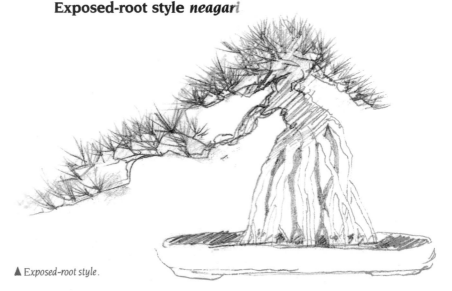

▲ *Exposed-root style.*

### Coiled style *bankan*

This is contrived by twisting leggy trunks into all sorts of coiled contortions. In my opinion it is an extremely perverse style (rarely seen these days) which bears little resemblance to trees in their typical state, although Scots pines and common junipers growing in thick heather can sometimes develop in this way naturally.

▶ *Coiled style.*

### Octopus style *takozukuri*

This describes the characteristics of many downward-trained, trailing, tentacle-like branches, sometimes referred to as helmet style and featured in many ancient parkland trees. A variation is to have several twisting trunks rising like tentacles from a single root base — looking a bit like an octopus.

▼ *Octopus style. This curiosity in Bonsai forms requires tentacle-like branches or trunks.*

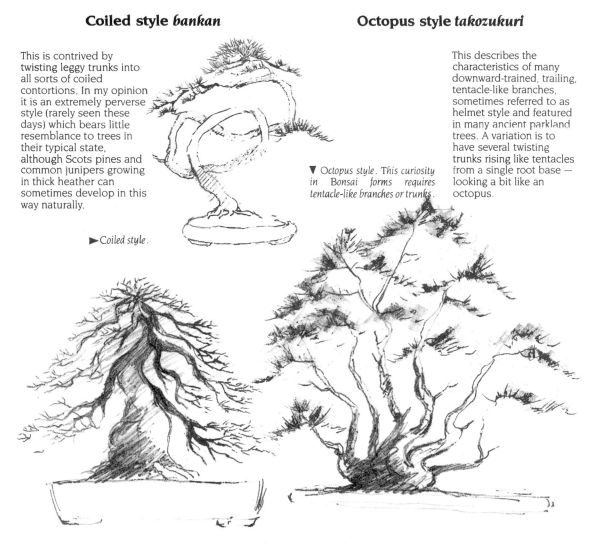

## Multi-trunk styles

### Twin-trunk style *sokan*

A multi-trunk variation in Bonsai styling which is the only instance of trees being planted in even numbers. (Multi-trunk styles traditionally progress as groups in arrangements of three, five, seven and nine. This is because it is usually easier to control the aesthetics with odd numbers and also because the Japanese who made this rule consider even-numbered arrangements to be unlucky). My own feeling is that if an actual count is necessary to determine whether there is an even or odd number of trees in any particular group then this is pushing the rule too far. If the group arrangement works satisfactorily in the visual sense then it should be perfectly acceptable irrespective of the number of trees in it.

The strict twin-trunk Bonsai description refers to trees that have a single root base with two trunks emanating from it. Ideally these trunks should divide as close to the ground as possible. Trees that begin as a single trunk, then divide several inches up should be avoided as these emerging trunks may well look more like two vertical pointing branches. It is also important that one of the trunks is thicker than the other to form a primary trunk and, again, it is important that when placing the tree in the pot one trunk is slightly forward of the other to strengthen the perspective. The tree should never be planted so that the two trunks are seen side by side as this tends to flatten the presentation. This is a very common fault with this style.

It does not really matter whether the primary trunk is forward or backward of the secondary trunk so long as the arrangement conveys a sense of depth. When there is a significant

► *The twin-trunk style should have trunks that divide as close to the soil level as possible and one trunk should be forward of the other.*

▲ *Mother and Son style trident maple from imported nursery stock trained since 1981; height 20 inches (52cm). This tree has a hollow trunk on the rear side.*

difference in the sizes of the two trunks the arrangement is often referred to as **Mother and Son** style. An endearing reference, typical of oriental sentiment.

Trees grown in the twin-trunk style are often tall and should be planted in long shallow pots or spacious slabs that enhance the tree's grandeur. Oval and rectangular glazed or unglazed pots are most

suitable. With less tall trees the same principles that govern aesthetic balance and harmony apply as with the earlier discussed styles. Always aim for an arrangement that creates an asymmetric triangle between tree and container.

A variation on this style is the **two-tree group** *soju* style. Again, apply similar aesthetic criteria with this variation as with the twin-trunk style.

► *Two-tree style larch collected from the wild as matchstick-thick seedlings about six inches (15cm) high. In training since 1975; height 30 inches (76cm).*

# Forest group style *yose-ue*

The multiplication of trunks increases in odd numbers with a numeric qualification for each until we reach nine or more trees which then qualify as a **forest group**.

Whatever the number of trees in a group it is vital to include a primary tree which has a greater height and trunk caliper than the others in the group. This provides a focal point. Again, try to inject a sense of expansiveness into the arrangement and ensure that the trees are placed in such a way that no more than two trees are positioned in a straight line. Vary the spaces between the trunks as equally spaced trunks would look very dull.

Stock trees should be selected with differing trunk thicknesses and if possible should all come from the same 'mother' plant so as to display identical characteristics. For example, similar leaf shape and size, bark surface, autumnal colour changes etc. This can easily be achieved by using air-layering techniques when propagating stock.

It is best to place the primary tree in a prominent position towards the front of the group with the remaining

▲ *Forest group style Japanese hornbeam from imported nursery stock trained since 1981; height 20 inches (50cm).*

trees diminishing in size and caliper towards the rear to improve the perspective. The result should inspire one's imagination to walk through the forest and explore its mysteries.

▲ Variations on group plantings to show satellite groups and other ways of interpreting the style. Shallow pots or slabs are essential for this style.

Forest group styles can be made from all sorts of tree-grouping configurations.

These can be single groups with no obvious intermediary paths, or groups made up from several smaller groupings suggesting open spaces or paths between the groups. In a design involving a major group with satellite groups, strictly speaking each of the satellite groups should have its own primary tree, and within the overall arrangement these primary trees should **each** differ in size and thickness.

Unlike single trees which need be considered only in respect of themselves, a forest group by definition involves several trees and therefore implies a scenic factor, so spacial punctuation between trees is critical if the design is to succeed. Forest group styles are a marvellous opportunity for using up surplus seedlings or cuttings which need not be very thick so long as there is some variation in the trunks, and convincing Bonsai can be produced in a season or two. Hedging trees available from garden centres are another quick way of obtaining stock, and species such as hornbeam, beech, hawthorn, Lonicera nitida are ideal. Other suitable species for forest groups are Japanese maples, zelkovas, junipers, pines, cryptomerias, spruces, laburnums etc.

Forest groups are invariably planted in ultra-shallow pots or slabs of slate etc to support the notion of the landscape, so lateral spread at ground level is most important to direct the eye in and around the forest.

Look into your forest group and listen awhile — can you hear the woodpecker drumming? If the Bonsai has succeeded you should be able to lose yourself in its miniature world.

## Multi-trunk variations

### Clump style *kabudachi*

This is essentially a multi-trunk tree whose trunks rise as a cluster from a single root base. Ideally the style demands a major trunk with several subsidiary trunks, and of course the branches should be arranged to produce an overall image rather than a series of separate trees. Trunks can be straight or have gentle curves built into them but do avoid trunks that appear like inverted frogs' legs and catapult prongs.

It is imperative that the trunks emerge from the root system as close to the soil surface as possible. An easy way to achieve this when starting off a clump is to find a suitable example of multiple branches (which can subsequently be turned into trunks) growing on a stock plant and to air-layer it. Very often these 'spoke-wheel' branches occur on maples and pines and whilst they may appear as faults in other applications, they are an ideal source for training when chosen with care.

Another way of obtaining material for this style is to use the residual trunk of a stock tree such as a trident maple which has been exhausted of cuttings and air-layerings. It can be pruned back to a point just above the root crown and this is best done in the peak of the growing season when the sap is rising vigorously. Several adventitious buds will appear around the cut area and in turn these will develop into shoots that can be trained into trunks suitable for clump style. Remember to allow one of the trunks to grow on more than the others so that it can be trained into a primary trunk. Keep in mind with clump style Bonsai that the image to be conveyed is one of multiple-trunks rather than multiple trees. Shallow, oval and rectangular pots are best for this style.

► *Clump style Japanese mountain maple (var. kyo hime). Imported as a semi-specimen tree and trained since 1982. Height approximately 27 inches (70cm).*

## Stump style *korabuki*

◄ *Stump style Bonsai — very rarely seen.*

A rarely-seen Bonsai style. Its only real difference from the clump style is that the root base from which the single or multiple trunks emerge is such an exaggerated mass it appears rather like a turtle's carapace. This effect can be achieved only with certain species of tree such as the trident maple and a few others that develop this bizarre root characteristic. It is a style that is best ignored as it is very difficult to present as a thing of beauty.

## Raft and sinuous styles

These styles are curious in that their 'trunks' have been created from branches. The original trunk is turned through ninety degrees and laid on its side, later to be buried under the soil. This reclining trunk or 'raft' needs to have all its branches removed from the underside and is then abrased underneath and treated with a rooting hormone compound to encourage it to produce roots along its whole length. When this has taken place, the original root system is pruned away.

Raft style *ikadabuki* differs from the Sinuous style *netsunagari* in that whilst the original trunk line of the raft remains in a straight line, the original trunk line of the sinuous is twisted into a series of curves. This is essentially to provide more depth to the arrangement which would otherwise tend to be rather flat and lack perspective. When

◀ Raft style is really a technique for producing a forest group. Remove all the branches from one side of the tree and treat cuts with a rooting hormone, then turn the tree through ninety degrees and plant in a suitable container, having first wired the remaining branches up to form the trunks of the group. When new roots form under the old trunk, the original root system can be cut off and the forest trained in the traditional manner.

considering Potensai for training into any style of Bonsai, do tilt the tree on its side to study the possibilities it may offer for either of the above styles, particularly if there is a predominance of branches on one side of the tree.

It is a curious fact when styling Bonsai that the more one is able to keep an open mind about it, the more likely one is to find a suitable solution. It is usually just a process of elimination. Consider first what you cannot train a Potensai into, and sooner or later an image will click in your mind's eye as you progress through the range of style possibilities and — wonder upon wonders — a masterpiece of creative innovation will be conceived.

◀ Sinuous style is similar to the raft style but has a winding raft base line instead of a straight base line which defines the true raft style. It is created in the same way as the raft but has its original trunk wired in a snaking manner as well as the branches that are to form the new trunks of the group. The advantage in this style over the raft is that a better sense of perspective can be achieved.

## Design elements

When designing the style of a Bonsai always consider it in respect of an asymmetric triangle or series of triangles and balance all the elements within the boundaries of this invisible reference frame. This will help to contain and harness the latent 'energies' or dynamics within the

design and make it easier to control and arrange the aesthetics of the design in a balanced and harmonious manner.

In planning the design, the roots, trunk, branches, twigs, foliage, flowers and fruit of the tree will need to be considered in relationship to one

another as well as in terms of their own abstract qualities. Shape, form, mass, line, tone, texture, colour, size, scale, contour etc all make a contribution to the final overall statement. Any aesthetic statement, whether it is a drawing, painting, sculpture, photograph or whatever,

will need to take these factors into consideration so develop an awareness as you create your Bonsai.

Another factor to consider is the size category that the Bonsai falls into. These are: large, usually over thirty inches (76cm); medium, about fifteen to thirty inches (38-76cm);

small or *shohin*, about six to fifteen inches (15-38cm); *mame* or bean-size Bonsai, which rarely exceed six inches (15cm) inclusive of pot.

Mame style Bonsai are often grown by specialists who are not interested in the larger sizes. The aesthetics governing their styling is the same as for larger trees but greater liberties can be taken in the choice of pots which are often very colourful and decorative. *Mame* Bonsai are fun to create and all Bonsai enthusiasts should try a few. Because they are so tiny their pots tend to dry out very quickly so it is best to stand them in seed trays containing damp peat.

▼ *Whenever possible design your Bonsai so that its major structure fits within an asymmetric triangle or triangles. This will make balancing the composition much easier.*

▼ *Mame Bonsai have a fascination all of their own. Like normal Bonsai they can be created from all sorts of species of trees and shrubs but varieties with small leaves are preferable. Because of their small size they will need some form of winter protection; a cold greenhouse would be ideal.*

# Basic training techniques

Dragonflies flashing
the lazy koi is gulping
high above a kite

Training is the general term we use when referring to the mechanical techniques deployed in controlling the aesthetics and form of the Bonsai. The two main areas for consideration are **pruning** and **wiring** techniques. These mechanical processes not only play a part in the shaping of the tree, but also support the horticultural dwarfing processes such as watering and feeding etc.

When training any tree certain priorities need to be taken into account. The first, and possibly most important, is to make sure your Potensai is healthy and vigorous in its growth. It is a living entity and unless this simple fact is respected and the tree nurtured accordingly the resultant Bonsai will never thrive.

We must always try to remember the responsibility we owe to our trees and never be in too much of a hurry to commence training.

Collected wildlings in particular need a period of rehabilitation. This can best be achieved by planting the tree in a large wooden box for a season or two and making sure it is well fed and watered to encourage vigorous growth, particularly at the root end of the tree. A good root system is vital to the well-being of the tree and although root pruning is one of the prime techniques used for dwarfing trees, this cannot be achieved without an established root system.

The next responsibility applies to the respective parts of the tree and the way to approach the pruning or wiring of each. These parts are: roots, trunk, primary branches, secondary branches, twigs, foliage, flowers and fruit.

# Pruning roots

Roots exist in a variety of forms to serve different functions. There are the large anchoring roots which develop to hold the tree firmly in the ground and prevent it from being blown over, and the finer secondary and hair roots that develop to take up the dissolved nutrients in the compost to other parts of the tree. The large roots should be pruned away at an early stage of training, leaving only the characterful surface roots that radiate from around the base of the trunk to form its buttress as well as a healthy rootball of secondary and hair roots. The basal surface roots

▲ *This beautiful example of radiating roots on a natural tree is what should be emulated when training Bonsai roots.*

make a major contribution to the illusion of age in the finished tree and should be carefully considered in their distribution and ramification. Sadly this is a much neglected aspect in contemporary Bonsai design and training and yet it needs as much attention as other parts of the tree. If possible, strive to improve on the root arrangement every time the tree is re-potted but

remember, if the process of untangling roots is likely to take a long time, then make sure the root system is sprayed frequently with water to prevent it from drying out.

The hair roots, which tend to be relatively short-lived, need frequent pruning to encourage the rejuvenation of new and active roots to maintain vigour in the tree. On average one third of the total root system should be pruned every time the tree is re-potted. Make sure all dead or rotting roots are also pruned out as these will only decompose and clog the airspaces in the

▲ *Surface roots on a silver birch Bonsai.*

compost and impede drainage.

Young developing trees require root pruning much more than mature Bonsai and if a tree has been extensively root pruned, the foliage of the tree will also need to be reduced to maintain a balance between the top and bottom ends of the tree, or the root system will become overworked and the tree may die as a result.

## Trunk

The trunk is pruned in respect of its specific style and to produce a good taper in it.

The technique is to over-grow the Potensai to increase caliper in the trunk and then to prune it back to a low branch which is then wired up to form a new trunk leader and the process repeated until the desired length is achieved. The size of the trunk will dictate the choice of tool for the job. For example, a chainsaw for very large trunks, a pruning saw for medium trunks, or a branch cutter, wen cutter etc. Whatever tool is used, make sure the cut is well finished off with a sharp knife to remove any burrs and treat it with a suitable sealant to protect it from disease and to facilitate healing.

The pruning of the trunk is often followed up immediately with wiring techniques to establish the tree's linear direction. 'Finding the line in Bonsai design' is a fascinating exercise and should never be rushed. Consider all the style possibilities before making any cuts.

◄ Trident maple grossly over-grown to approximately ten feet (3m) in height to thicken the trunk.

▲ Large branches roughly sawn with a chainsaw.

◄ Roughly pruned areas should be close pruned with an electric reciprocating saw or sharp hand-pruning saw, then trimmed back with a very sharp knife and finally chiselled back to a concave dish shape to improve callousing.

► This tiny little shoot will be trained into the new trunk leader and the whole process repeated until the right length and taper of trunk is achieved. The branch pointing up to the right is retained only to keep the tree alive. It too will be pruned out in time. The branches can be developed at a later date.

## Primary branches

Frequently these branches are structurally pruned when the main trunk line is being considered and it is usual to wire them into place at the same time. This is best executed in spring or autumn for most species and if extensive pruning is undertaken then protect against frost during the immediate following winter, especially for the genetic dwarf varieties of pine such as *Pinus sylvestris, var. Beuvronensis*.

The primary branches are the main axial branches which originate directly from some point of the trunk. They are the branches that form the first, second, back, third, fourth branch etc on the tree and it is from these that the secondary branches and twigs ramify. They are the 'arms' of the tree that carry the 'clouds' of foliage and their positions and structure will often determine the character of the tree and its visual density and texture. When pruning these branches due consideration needs to be given to this and the spaces between them so as to produce a sense of harmony without monotony.

*▼ A typical container-grown Scots pine (var.Beuvronensis). The tree has been closely inspected to determine its best potential for Bonsai training.*

*▼ It has been decided to use two of the lower branches as second and third trunks. Note how the main trunk has been pruned back at the top to allow a thinner branch to continue the trunk line. This will improve the trunk's taper.*

*▼ The tree has been completely wired using several different gauges of wire. The three trunks differ in height to generate a hierarchy of primary, secondary and tertiary levels and lead fishing weights have been used to bend the delicate top branches. When structuring a Bonsai initially it is usual to wire virtually every part of the tree in order to relate all of its elements. This is especially the case with pines. It sometimes takes two or three days to wire a large or complicated tree.*

## Secondary branches and twigs

The secondary branches are those that emanate laterally and alternately from the primary branches and they should be pruned to form lozenge-shaped saucers for the foliage clouds. The twigs are the fine foliage-bearing branches that grow up from these secondary branches and their pruning is usually a seasonal exercise in grooming to improve the peripheral outlines and contours of the tree.

When pruning branches, bear in mind not only the aesthetics of the arrangement but also the position of the branch in terms of the ventilation and light that it will receive. This is most important as both these factors actively contribute to the health and well-being of the tree.

## Foliage

◄ A Japanese mountain maple in spring shortly after the leaves have hardened off. It is in good health and full of vigour.

▲ The same tree with virtually every leaf pruned off leaving only a portion of stem behind. Feed and water very sparingly after pruning or the purpose of the exercise will be defeated and the tree will develop large leaves again.

▼ The same tree in the early autumn. The new leaves are now smaller and in good colour. This pruning technique can be repeated each year on young trees. Mature trees should not be pruned in this way as they do not have the same degree of vigour to withstand the shock.

Foliage needs to be pruned for cosmetic reasons — usually to reduce the visual mass, and when a deciduous tree is obviously vigorous in its growth the leaves can be totally pruned out, leaving only a portion of the stem. After about three weeks this stem will dry up and drop off and the axial bud at its base will develop into a more refined shoot with smaller leaves that tend to display better autumn colour. This practice of leaf pruning is best done in early summer just after the first flush of leaves have hardened off.

If the tree is at all weak or lacking in vigour do not prune the leaves as this is where photosynthesis takes place: light energy is converted into chemical energy to form sugars and starches and other beneficial products necessary for the development of the roots and other parts of the tree. The leaves in a sense can be likened to mini-factories and their role is crucial, so to prune them just for the sake of it could be disastrous.

▲ *Unless a tree is required for an exhibition or to photograph, it makes sense to let it enjoy a period of uninhibited growth from time to time so that its vigour will improve and it can capitalize on the effects of photosynthesis.*

▲ *When the tree is eventually pruned, trim the twigs etc in respect of the tree's style, and aim to create an overall visual harmony.*

▼ *When a tree is pruned certain branches are occasionally left to grow on to enable them to thicken and also to thicken the trunk section below them. Eventually they too will be pruned in keeping with the general shape of the tree.*

# Flowers and fruit

A number of species offer this attractive bonus. Trees such as quince, crab apple, cotoneasters, wisteria, azaleas, cherries, blackthorns etc. It is unusual to prune off the flowers unless the tree is disproportionately overloaded. When this is the case, a few of the flowers can be removed, particularly with varieties such as azaleas. On the other hand it is often necessary to remove a number of the fruits to balance off the visual effect and, more importantly, to reduce some of the workload on the rest of the tree.

A large number of fruits on a tree may prove a novelty talking point but the demand it makes on the resources of the tree is often excessive and, without thinning out, is likely to result in the death of the tree the following spring.

The photographs and drawings illustrate a wide range of pruning techniques.

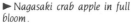

► Nagasaki crab apple in full bloom.

▼ The same tree in autumn with a rich crop of fruit. Unfortunately the fruit was left on for too long which overtaxed the tree's reserves and it died the following spring. After a week or two's enjoyment of ripened fruit, it would probably be wise to prune out about two-thirds of the crop.

# Wiring

The application of wire to parts of the tree is an essential aid to the structuring and shaping processes. There are numerous mechanical variations as the illustrations show and ample opportunities for improvisation and innovation.

Whatever techniques are chosen skilful application is important. There is no excuse for slovenly workmanship in the application of wire and nothing more unsightly than when it is witnessed in practice. When wire is used for training purposes it is likely to be in place for six to eighteen months or more so every effort should be taken to make it as tidy a job as possible.

The purpose of wiring is usually to induce a part of the tree to adopt a new position for visual enhancement or corrective reasons. The best wire to use for this is aluminium wire, in a variety of gauges. The next best is annealed copper wire.

Copper wire can be annealed by heating it to a cherry-red colour in a straw or wood fire and allowing it to cool. It will then be softened and much easier to wrap around the branches. This wrapping process will change the molecular structure of the wire, hardening it, and it will subsequently retain its new position. Do not use copper wire on prunus species as it is poisonous to them and will kill the wired section.

Wiring is mostly applied in the initial stages of structuring a Bonsai but it will continue to a lesser degree throughout the life of the tree, so mastering the technique of wiring really is a necessary evil.

When wiring, use both hands and try not to rock the tree too much in its pot as this will damage the roots. Ideally the angle of the wire to the part that is to be wired should be approximately forty-five degrees. Try to match the gauge of wire to the caliper of branch to be wired and, if it is insufficient to hold it in position, use a second piece of wire immediately parallel to the first and in contact with it.

▲ *This willow has just been pruned after a year's unchecked growth.*

◀ *It has since been grown on for two months and then thinned out. All the remaining branches have been wired to create a weeping effect. These wires will be left on (even if the tree is to be shown), until the end of the growing season when they will then be removed. The exercise will be repeated annually: ie prune, grow, thin out, wire, prune again etc. In general if there is any risk of damage to the bark when removing wire from branches or trunk it would be better to cut it off rather than to try unwinding it.*

Always make sure the starting point of the wire is well anchored or the operation will be abortive, and to finish the exercise use a jinning tool to wrap the last loop as there will be insufficient leverage to bend the wire manually.

Avoid leaving protruding lengths of wire at the ends of branches as these are unsightly and can be a hazard to the eyes.

All sorts of clamps, tensioners, weights and templates can be used in support of, or as alternatives to, wiring and the illustrations show some variations.

You will find that if wire is left on a trunk or branch for too long it is likely to bite into the bark causing unsightly scarring. This is not too bad on coniferous species which will usually heal over in time but on deciduous species, such as beech or zelkova, the scarring is likely to be permanent. Always keep a watchful eye for this problem and remove the wire immediately you see it happening. If the branch moves back, then replace the wire in a slightly different position until the branch has 'set'.

Any tree that has been excessively pruned and wired will benefit from winter protection by being placed in a cold glasshouse or equivalent.

Finally, when you have decided to wire a tree, it makes sense to stop all watering for a day or two beforehand. This will lower the turgidity (swelling with moisture) in the tree causing the branches to become slightly limp and therefore less likely to snap when bent. However, do not be too enthusiastic in this practice or the tree is likely to be droughted and will die.

▲ Prune and wire branches to form lozenge-shaped foliage clouds and when grooming be sure to remove all downward-pointing needles or leaves except of course with weeping styles like willows, tamarisks, wisterias and so on.

▶ The major trunk in this two-trunk style larch is leaning too much to the left and this needs correcting.

▼ 'Worm's eye' view of branches. Notice how the secondary branches have been spread to form saucer shapes and the finer twigs trained upwards to support the foliage. Not only is this aesthetically satisfying but it is ideal for catching light which is essential for photosynthesis.

▶ With the use of a suitable clamp the fault can be remedied. If the clamp is likely to be in position for a long period of time, wrap some protective foam plastic around the trunk where it comes in contact with the clamp.

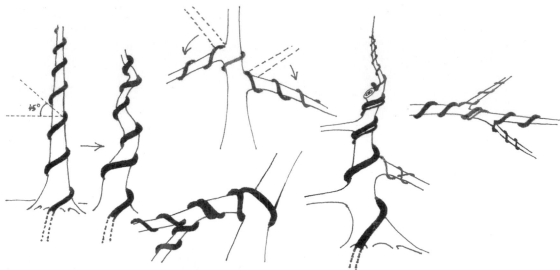

▲ Variations on wiring. Whenever possible, wire should pass around the convex side of the trunk or branch that is being bent in order to minimize any tendency for the branch to snap. If one piece of wire is used for two branches, it has a better anchoring effect. Select the gauge of wire to suit the caliper of branch to be bent and change it as necessary. Wire should be wrapped at forty-five degrees to the axial line of the branch. Make sure when wiring from the soil upwards that it is firmly anchored in the soil.

▲ A loop of wire placed over the branch and under a piece of wire attached to the pot can be tightened with a tommy bar to lower the branch to the desired position. Again use protective foam plastic.

◄ Trees in group plantings can be braced together for support by strapping lengths of spliced bamboo between the trunks.

▼ Before wiring thickish branches, it is a good idea to cut a slit through the bark about two inches (5cm) long below the point of greatest tension and down to the sap wood. The healing scar has a restrictive effect on the branch causing it to remain more firmly in position.

▲ A chain strapped to a belt which in turn is wrapped around the pot provides 360 degrees of anchoring points to which branches can be tied.

▲ A crude method for training willow branches in order to form the branch arches at the top of the tree. Once they set, the long branches will be pruned away and new ones grown in their place. These in turn will be wired in the traditional way.

▼ If wire is left on a branch for too long it can bite deeply into the bark leaving very unsightly scars which are difficult, if not impossible, to eradicate at a later date. Always keep an eye open for this problem and remove wire as soon as the fault appears.

▲ When wiring heavy branches it is best to cut right the way through the branch before applying wire. This can be done with an appropriately sized branch-splitting tool. Besides reducing the tendency to break, the healing tissues cause the branch to set better.

# Pruning pines

There are basically three different pruning techniques that apply to pines: structural pruning, refinement pruning and generative pruning. Generally speaking, structural pruning and refinement pruning require similar aesthetic and horticultural considerations as are applied to most species of tree and they are dealt with elsewhere in the book. Generative pruning is something quite different, however, and is specific to pines and some other conifers. Its purpose is to generate and increase the production of vegetative buds on the tree.

With pines the normal pattern of growth is for the tree to produce an apical (tip) bud at the end of each branch and at the top of the trunk leader with two or three secondary buds surrounding it. Unless this growth pattern is interrupted, there is no reason for it to behave in any other way. This is not an ideal situation as the internodal distance in the shoot length between buds is usually too long and subsequently difficult to train in a pleasing and suitable way. It tends to produce 'lollipops' of foliage at the ends of each shoot. This problem can be overcome.

In most varieties of pine each pair of needles has a rudimentary eye bud at its base and this is the bud we need to activate. It is too small to see and requires a powerful magnifying glass or microscope to make it visible. Normally it would remain dormant and fall off with the seasonal abscission of the needles, according to the species, unless the shoot was threatened or wounded in some way.

Pruning is interpreted by the tree as a threatening act and causes it to release certain auxins (organic substances) which in turn trigger off a reaction in the pruned shoot. This reaction manifests itself by causing several of the eye buds to develop into normal buds which in turn produce vegetative shoots. Concurrent with this botanical phenomenon is the further production of numerous adventitious buds on bare branches of up to five years of age and sometimes even more.

The increase in buds developed in this way is a huge advantage in the

◀ This mountain pine has had its roots trained over the rock for nearly twelve years. It is now ready for structural pruning.

▶ It is usual to prune the lower branches first then gradually work up the tree. Wrap wire around the primary branches first, then around the secondary branches.

◀ Carefully bend the branches into position.

▶ The same tree completely pruned and wired. When pruning for structure, it is necessary to be quite radical in order to establish the major axial lines and basic form of the Bonsai. The finer twigs that will support the clouds of foliage can be developed next and they in turn will need to be refined over the following two years and the Bonsai planted into a more appropriate pot.

▲ This Japanese black pine (P. thunbergii) has already been structurally pruned and wired in the informal upright style. It has been watered and fed well for a couple of seasons to encourage vigour and ample growth. It is now ready for its initial refinement pruning.

▲ The tree has had its foliage extensively thinned out and several of the shoots have been pruned back to form related contours. It fits snugly within an asymmetric triangle. Notice how the foliage in the crown has been reduced much more than in the lower branches. This will cause the lower branches to strengthen and it will also thicken the trunk immediately below them. The oversized pot is used only for training. The trunk is too parallel and needs to be thickened in its lower region.

▲ Trunks can be encouraged to thicken by very gently tapping the bark so as to bruise the underlying cellular structure. As this repairs itself it will swell in the process causing the trunk to thicken. Only hammer one side of the trunk at a time. Continue the process over the next few months or years until the desired girth is reached.

◄ A typical arrangement of primary and secondary buds at the end of an unpruned shoot.

► Here there are 'lollipops' of foliage at the ends of several of the branches. This tree is in need of generative pruning to encourage more adventitious buds to develop on denuded branches so that better foliage contours can be incorporated into its design.

► This sketch shows observations through a microscope of a pair of pine needles. The embryonic eye bud is located at the base of each pair of needles. This little bud is potentially crucial for pine Bonsai development, and stimulating buds of this sort to grow is the basis of each of the following generative pruning techniques. Each technique will need to be studied very carefully as each in turn triggers off a subtly different growth pattern.

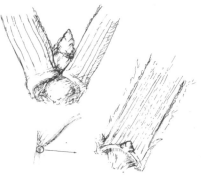

creation of pine Bonsai as it provides much denser growth. The illustrations that follow demonstrate a variety of techniques that can be employed.

However, it is important that pines destined for any of these pruning techniques are first grown to encourage maximum health and vigour. Failure to obey this 'rule' is likely to result in the tree suffering irreparable damage to the pruned areas, or even dying. Although having said this, pines are generally very resilient trees.

At face value, a number of the techniques will appear to be very similar but when studied closely their subtle differences will be apparent. The timing of the pruning is also important as it will affect the final result and cause

the residual buds to be larger or smaller as the case may be. In order that these pruning techniques can be used in the southern as well as northern hemispheres, I have made use of seasons rather than months to indicate the best time to prune.

Each pruning sequence illustrated here shows what might be achieved from the same shoot in any given season if one or other of the techniques is applied to it. It is important to establish exactly what the objective is before applying any one of the pruning methods as the net result will differ in each case.

It is perfectly in order to apply different techniques to different parts of the tree in the same growing season if this is appropriate.

▲ *The formation of eye buds in between some of the pairs of needles and also the production of adventitious buds on older wood can clearly be seen in this photograph. They have resulted from one of the generative pruning techniques. The number of buds likely to be produced is unpredictable but if the tree is healthy and vigorous the chance of more buds is probable.*

**Objective**
*To increase the length of the branches and the girth of the trunk and to improve the root production.*

**Technique**
*Do not prune new shoots. Feed and water well in the growing season and provide ample sunlight. Best used in conjunction with field-grown Potensai.*

**Comment**
*Applied mostly with young potential Bonsai to promote maximum growth and also occasionally to extend branch length.*

**Objective**
*To maintain the tree's size and outline with minimal growth.*

**Technique**
*Remove the apical (tip) bud and all but two of the lateral buds before active growth begins. Half-pinch candles when they are approximately one inch (25mm) long.*

**Comment**
*This is an ideal technique for mature specimen trees. Feed and water very sparingly during the growing season to keep needle growth down to a minimum.*

### Objective
A grooming technique to increase shoot density and improve the contours of the foliage clouds.

### Technique
Pinch out two thirds of the candle before needles elongate. This is usually in late spring.

### Comment
Feed and water normally. Next season's buds will be an average size. This technique is suitable for trees already well structured and with ample branches.

### Objective
To increase the bud production on trees with normal growth.

### Technique
Pinch out the candles when new needles are approximately 3/8 inch to 1/2 inch (10-12mm) long and not yet hardened. This is usually in the late spring or early summer.

### Comment
The new buds are small to average and usually abundant. Adventitious buds often occur on older wood. Next year's growth will be 'tighter'. Feed and water as normal. This is a useful way to increase twigginess.

### Objective
To reduce needle length and increase bud production on **very vigorously** growing trees that were well fertilized the previous year.

### Technique
Remove apical and lateral buds at their points of origin when the candles are one inch (25mm) long. This is usually early in the growing season.

### Comment
Smaller adventitious buds soon form at the terminal end of the branch and sometimes in the leaf bases. A number of these buds will develop rapidly enough to produce tight growth with short needles in the same growing season. The remainder will grow the following year. Do not practice this technique for more than two consecutive years or weakening of the tree may result.

### Objective
To improve root production and thicken the caliper on trunk and branches, to produce **very small** buds on young trees and also to extend branch length.

### Technique
Feed and water well during the growing season allowing unchecked growth. Prune back new shoots in late summer/ autumn leaving three to four pairs of needles on each shoot.

### Comment
**Very small** buds will develop over the winter, producing short needles with next year's growth if minimal watering is given. A useful technique to employ every third or fourth year.

### Objective
To make use of the current season's growth and the effects of photosynthesis and to produce **small buds** from the eye buds left in the residual sheaths.

### Technique
Allow candles to grow unchecked for the whole of the growing season; water and feed well.

Remove **all** the current season's needles very carefully by pulling them out, **one at a time** and not in pairs. A small percentage of eye buds will remain in some of the needle sheaths. Shorten the shoots to the desired length by finger pinching. This technique should be executed immediately after the needles have ripened.

### Comment
Timing is critical and the technique is best practised over one to three weeks to increase the chances of success. The results are unpredictable but good if timed correctly. Adventitious buds also form on older wood.

### Objective
As above

### Technique
With a pair of scissors, cut all the current season's needles just above the needle sheaths in **late summer** after the needles have fully ripened. Prune back residual shoots to the desired length.

### Comment
A little more predictable than the last technique but it can leave unsightly brown tips where the needles have been trimmed. This technique is therefore more suited to younger trees at an early stage of training where the appearance of brown tips is unimportant.

### Objective
To improve root production and thicken trunk and branches but this time with **minimal branch elongation**. It will also increase foliage density.

### Technique
Allow full seasonal growth with normal watering and feeding. Prune back shoots to their point of origin in the **early autumn**.

### Comment
**Small buds** will appear in the following spring. Note, when this technique is employed, any long needles will also have been removed bringing the tree more or less back to its former state which makes it a useful 'containing' technique.

### Objective
To produce intermediary bud break between lengthy internodal shoots.

### Technique
With a very sharp scalpel cut through the bark and down to the sapwood immediately below each pair of needles in late summer after the needles have ripened.

### Comment
This wounding action will inhibit the passage of auxins etc flowing down from the needles and result in a number of the eye buds developing at the base of each needle sheath. Rub out any unwanted buds. This is a painstaking exercise that is not recommended for the impatient. Removal of the apical and lateral buds at the time of 'surgery' will increase the chances of success and will improve the production of bud generating auxins.

◀ A 'leggy' inter-nodal shoot having the bark cut to the sapwood under each pair of needles with a sharp scalpel to stimulate bud production. (This is the last technique in the series.)

▶ The same shoot the following year showing numerous buds that would not otherwise have developed.

## The jin

A jin is a dead branch or portion of trunk (usually the top) that has had the bark removed. (If this is being done artificially, never remove bark to a point where the life of the tree is endangered.)

In nature jins occur mainly on mature and ancient trees and as a result of hostile situations and inclement weather. The batterings of wind, frost, ice and sandstorms cause erosion of the bark and expose the underlying wood. Insect and fungal attack may also play a part. The wood dries and is gradually bleached by the sun to an attractive silvery-grey colour.

Because jins are invariably associated with old age and austere conditions, this should be the first consideration when creating a jin. Study natural jins carefully and endeavour to reconstruct these phenomena with care and sensitivity. It would be pointless to create a jin on a young sapling or on branches

that are too thin. Remember, the removal of bark reduces branch caliper to the point where too thin a jin would look ridiculous and would not appear convincing. So relate the caliper of the jin to the mass of the trunk in order to maintain a sense of proportion. Jins should be considered only if they are going to enhance the illusion of age and maturity on a Bonsai and should not be executed just for the sake of it. When well sculpted they bring majesty to the tree and in a way release its 'soul'; they suggest a timelessness and often inspire a sense of awe.

Jins are usually associated with coniferous species as they tend to occur naturally in the more inhospitable regions and at relatively high altitudes. Deciduous species are usually more lush as they grow in the lowlands, plains and valleys. Nevertheless deciduous trees do sometimes display jins in the higher

reaches of the tree — often as a result of a lightning strike.

When creating a jin it is more convincing if the bark or wood is torn or ripped back on itself with a jinning tool or pair of pliers. This is better than carving it with a knife which can produce a sharpened-pencil effect. Splitting the end of the branch longitudinally with a branch side-cutting tool makes it easier to start the tearing action. The residual wood fibres that result from this tearing action can be burnt off with a jeweller's blowlamp or scraped away with bits of glass from broken bottles. Their curved edges are ideally suited for the purpose, but watch your fingers!

After creating the jin, you should allow it to dry for a few weeks and then treat it with lime sulphur solution which helps preserve the wood and bleaches it to an attractive silvery-grey colour. A little

soot mixed with the solution helps mellow the jin and give it the appearance of great age. Lime sulphur is bright yellow when first applied but soon changes to white.

Jins are dramatic features of some Bonsai and can often provide a useful focal point or add to the association of ideas in support of the tree's style. For example, a tall upright sequoia may have its crown jinned out to suggest it has been struck by lightning; a windswept style Bonsai might well have its image strengthened by a few strategically positioned jins; or a jin may suggest that the original trunk has died as a result of old age or elemental damage and that a younger branch has grown up to form a new crown. This is the 'storyline' behind the beech-jinning sequence of photographs shown in this section.

Jins are best used in conjunction with *sharis* which are discussed next.

▶ *This beech was collected from an old hedge and brought to one of my workshops by a Bonsai student for styling and structuring. It had a complicated multi-trunk crown which needed simplifying. The trunk was stocky with well-defined bark which begged to be shown to advantage. It was therefore decided to make this the main feature of the tree. The sketch shows the projected image of a coastline windswept tree, suggesting that the original trunk on the upper right has died at some earlier age and that a new crown has developed, with branch lines all favouring a left-hand direction. Not only does this imply the wind direction but also introduces a visual movement into the tree, lending it a dynamic appearance. The repeated lines and flattened crown increase the illusion of age, establishing the Bonsai as a tree rather than a bush.*

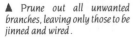

▲ Prune out all unwanted branches, leaving only those to be jinned and wired.

▲ Draw a line with a felt-tip pen to show where the jin is to end.

▶ Saw half-way through the back of the branches to be jinned, slightly higher up the tip of each jin

►Using the handles of a large branch side-cutting tool (or equivalent) to help leverage, bend forward and break the branch.

◄ These broken branches appear more natural than if they had been carved with a knife: use a jinning tool or a pair of pliers and work all around the branch by gripping the end with the tool and ripping the bark back down the branch. Carve away any remaining bark to the drawn line and scrape away any remaining bark to the drawn line and scrape away any remaining wood fibres with bits of glass from broken bottles or burn off with a jeweller's blow-lamp. It may be easier to perform this latter task at a later date when the jin has dried out. Gentle rubbing with sandpaper will finally give the jin a convincing weathered look. With larger jins it may be necessary to modify the form of the jin by carving it with an electric drill fitted with a flexi-ble lead and a variety of shaped burr bits and rasps (obtainable from most tool shops).

▲ Leave the jins to dry for a few weeks then paint them with a solution of lime sulphur to pre-serve and bleach the wood.

►This is how the tree looks after it has been pruned, wire-trained and re-potted. The branch on the right of the trunk needs to develop a little more before it is wired to its final position.

▲ *Windswept style larch with jins
and sharis.*

Like the jin, the shari is a part of the tree that has had its bark removed. And whereas the jin is specific to branches, the shari is specific to the trunk or parts of it. Its preparation is very similar to that of the jin but there are two points that must be remembered. Firstly, when removing bark from the trunk make sure you do not remove any that is below the soil surface or it is likely to rot. Secondly, make sure that enough bark is left on the trunk to supply the living parts of the tree with nutrients.

As the scale of the trunk is much greater than that of

## The shari

the branches you will need to use suitably matched tools, which may include: chainsaws, power drills fitted with rasps, power routers, chisels and gouges.

Like the jin, the shari is to enhance, age and generate a sense of awe and austerity in the Bonsai. It is best achieved with mature trees and more often with coniferous species — particularly with the needle juniper J.*rigida*. When creating a shari with

a deciduous species you might consider combining it with a hollowed-out trunk. This is often witnessed in nature with oaks and chestnuts and can give the Bonsai an added dimension.

All external surfaces that have been stripped of bark should be treated with a solution of lime sulphur to preserve and bleach the wood. Internal surfaces, as with hollow-trunked trees, should have an abundance of soot added

to the solution in order to achieve a darkened effect. A bleached-out hollow trunk would look very unnatural.

As with a jin do not create a shari unless it really is going to enhance the overall image of the Bonsai because any bark that is removed from the tree cannot be replaced and irreparable damage can result if the exercise is unsuccessful. On the other hand, well-executed sharis can give a Bonsai a sense of power and majesty.

Sharis are mostly associated with the driftwood style of Bonsai.

## Lime sulphur recipe

To one and a half pints of water (.8 litre) add two ounces (57 grams) of hydrated garden lime and bring to the boil stirring slowly.

Add three ounces (85 grams) of flowers of sulphur a little at a time and make sure the solution is stirred continuously and kept

on a gentle boil.

After a little while the sulphur will disappear and the liquid will turn a yellowish-brown colour.

The lime will take a little longer to dissolve, often leaving some undissolved. When it appears that no more is going to dissolve,

allow the solution to cool, then drain off the liquid and filter it through an old nylon stocking into storage bottles.

When painted on to jins and sharis this solution will preserve and bleach them. It is bright yellow at first but soon changes to white.

It is very important that the above action takes place out of doors and in a well ventilated part of the garden as the fumes are most unpleasant and may well be toxic.

Do make sure lime sulphur is kept out of the reach of children and, as a precaution, mark it with a poison label.

◄ *This container-grown twin-trunk cypress was brought along to one of my Bonsai workshops and after much examination and discussion we decided to de-bark one of the trunks totally to form a shari with several jins.*

► *The same tree about three hours later. The sketch was provided for the student to use as reference. When the denuded wood is dry, after about three months, it will be treated with lime sulphur to bleach the wood and preserve it. And in a season or two's time, it will be safe to re-pot it.*

# Propagation

*Pine resin scenting
the primal forests shrivel
log fires crackle warm*

The various methods of propagation discussed in this chapter should be considered as an addition to the Bonsai sources referred to in Chapter Two.

Each propagation method — from seed, from cuttings, from graftings and from layerings — follows similar routines associated with normal horticultural practice and the suggestions proffered can be extended by referring to any book on horticultural propagation — of which there are plenty.

Propagation from seed can be a very long-winded way of producing Bonsai but if the seedlings are planted in a garden bed to grow on for a few seasons the process can be accelerated and some very fine trees produced. One of the problems with growing from seed is that the progeny are not guaranteed to be true to type as hybridization may have taken place when the

seed was fertilized. This problem is overcome when propagating from cuttings, and provided one uses the same 'mother' plant, the progeny will be identical in character. This is particularly useful when making forest groups.

Most plants can be propagated from cuttings but there are some that are notoriously difficult —

especially pines and a number of the coniferous varieties. When this is the case, the best method would be to use a grafting technique. However, one of the major disadvantages of grafting is that ugly scars can form at the point of union. Nevertheless grafting is sometimes the only way certain species can be propagated. For instance, many genetic dwarf

species that result from 'witches's brooms' cannot be grown in any other way as they require vigorous root stocks to sustain them and are often incapable of growing well on their own root systems.

Layering, in particular air-layering, is a very useful method of producing excellent material for Bonsai training and this method is covered in great detail. Many of my own favourite Bonsai began as a result of air-layering.

◀ *Typical 'witches' broom' growing on a Scots pine in the Ashdown forest, Sussex, England. Its characteristics are almost identical to the cultivar, Beuvronensis. I have managed to make a number of successful grafts from this sport which I have named Pinus sylvestris, var. Dansai. At the moment I am growing the grafts on to form mother plants from which further grafts can be made.*

◀ *Japanese grey-bark elm grown from seed planted in 1972, about eleven years old when the photograph was taken.*

## Seeds

Always purchase seed from a reputable seedsman to ensure the seed is viable and store carefully according to the instructions on the pack. Many varieties of trees require their seeds to be stratified in order to break dormancy and begin the process of germination. To do this, you need to mix the seeds with about three times their volume in damp sand or peat and then place this mixture in a polythene bag in the refrigerator over the winter period. Be sure to inspect the bag frequently and, as soon as there are signs of

germination, the seeds should be planted into seed pans with a suitable seed compost. I use the 'sievings' from my basic Mark one compost (see page 28) that has passed through a one-eighths inch (3mm) sieve and is too fine for normal Bonsai use. This is an ideal medium for seed propagation.

Seed should be planted in clean wooden or plastic seed pans that have ample drainage holes. Place a substrata of drainage crocks or coarse grit over the base of the pan to a depth of about half an inch (12mm) and then add the seed compost. This should be about two inches (5cm) in depth and the top should be evenly tamped down with a flat piece of wood.

Sprinkle, or individually plant the seed on the surface and cover with additional compost to a depth of twice the height of the seed. Now water the seed by standing the container in a larger pan of water until the water reaches the surface of the compost and then remove the container carefully so as not to disturb the soil. Cover the compost with a sheet of brown paper to reduce the light level and to absorb heat and then place a sheet of glass over the pan, completely covering it. (Alternatively conduct the same procedure in a mini plastic propagating 'glasshouse' made for the purpose and available from any garden store.)

Place the seed pan in a shaded part of a cold glasshouse or protected part of the garden. Remove the glass covering and brown paper from time to time to check whether any of the seeds have germinated and as soon as this begins, take the coverings off permanently. Never allow the compost to dry out but at the same time do not over water as this can cause rot at the base of the seedlings and kill them. Make sure the seedlings are kept out of draughts but well ventilated.

When the seedlings have produced their first pair of true leaves, they can be carefully transplanted into suitable pots of about three inches (75mm) in diameter. Make sure careful attention is paid to spreading out the roots. It would also be sensible to prune off the tip of the tap root before planting the seedling. This will increase the production of radial roots. The seedlings should be grown on in these pots for a season and then transplanted to a garden bed where they can be developed to whatever size is required. Again, make sure the roots are well spread when planting. By growing on in this way one can increase trunk girth very rapidly and when the tree has reached the desired size, it can be dug up and planted into a large wooden box or pot where training can begin.

Species that are well suited to propagation from seed are: zelkova, cotoneaster, acer, birch, ginkgo, larch, pine and pomegranate.

## Cuttings

Cuttings are a simple and inexpensive way of generating material for Bonsai. There are several advantages to be gained over propagation from seed. The first is that there will be no tap root. Another is that the progeny will be guaranteed identical if the cuttings are made from the same 'mother' plant, which is obviously useful if one wishes to be exact with nomenclature — and if identical material for multiple plantings is required this is a good way of producing it.

Most species can be propagated from cuttings but some, particularly pines, can be very difficult. The Japanese black pine P. *thunbergii* and the Japanese white pine P. *parviflora, var. zui-sho* are exceptions. Even if pine cuttings could be made to root, it does not follow that they will thrive on their own roots. Most pine varieties need to be grafted for best results.

Volumes have already been written on propagation of plant material in innumerable books so I will concentrate purely on my own experiences. I find that for the pine species mentioned above, the best time to start the cuttings is in February or just before the plants emerge from dormancy. For most deciduous varieties the best time is just after the current season's shoots have ripened. This is usually around late June.

For pines, cut two to three inch (5-8cm) lengths of the previous year's terminal shoots and remove a third of the needles from the base end. With a sharp sterilized knife cut the base to form an asymmetric 'V'. Dip the cutting into a solution of rooting hormone gel or dust with rooting hormone powder and plant in a seed tray containing two inches (5cm) of seed compost as described in the section on propagating from seed above. Water carefully by drenching with a spray and place in a humid environment such as a propagating house. If subterranean heat can be supplied and the humidity maintained by a mist unit, the chances of success are heightened. Never allow the cuttings to dry out but at the same time do not over water. Every now and again lift the odd cutting to check whether it has rooted. As soon as the majority have rooted, transplant them into three-inch (75mm) diameter pots and grow on for a season or two before planting into a large wooden box or garden bed to gain size. When the cutting has achieved the desired size

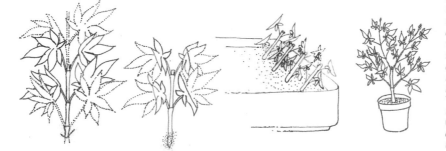

▲ *Cuttings of deciduous species are best made just after the current season's growth has ripened. This is usually in early summer. Remove the growing tip and leave only two pairs of leaves. With a sharp knife cut the base just below a node to an asymmetric 'V'. Trim back leaves to half size to reduce transpiration and workload and then dip them in a rooting hormone powder or gel. Plant them at an angle in a seed tray filled with equal parts of peat and sand. Water carefully so as not to disturb the compost and place in a humid environment providing heat from beneath if possible. When the cuttings have rooted transplant them into three inch (75mm) diameter pots and grow on for a season. To accelerate trunk development plant out in a garden bed for two to three years.*

transplant it into a suitable pot and train as appropriate.

With deciduous cuttings and most other coniferous varieties, such as spruce, larch, juniper etc, cut lengths of ripened current season's growth. Deciduous species should have the terminal shoot pinched out and the cutting reduced to two pairs of leaves. In the case of large-leaved species such as quince, beech, hornbeam etc, the leaves should be cut in half to reduce transpiration. Coniferous cuttings should be reduced to about two inches (5cm) by cutting back the base end (leave the terminal buds intact) and some of the lower needles or leaves should be removed. In both cases the base of the cutting should be cut to an asymmetric 'V' and

▶ *Grey-bark elm forest group made from cuttings.*

treated in a similar manner to the pine cuttings described above.

It makes good sense to spray the cuttings with a proprietory fungicide occasionally to reduce any tendency to rot.

Unless winter protection can be provided for the cuttings, it is best to leave the cuttings in the seed tray until the following spring when they can be transplanted. Some cuttings will take many months before they show any signs of rooting. Provided they are not dead (and this is indicated by the cutting turning brown), just persevere and in time roots should form.

Suitable species from which cuttings can be taken are: mountain and trident maple, Arctic birch, cotoneaster, cryptomeria, cypress, Chinese and other forms of elm, ficus, firethorn, ginkgo, Lonicera nitida, hornbeam, jasmine, juniper, myrtle, Japanese black pine, potentilla, quince, azalea and rhododendron, serrisa, spiraea, spruce, tamarisk, sequoia, willow and possibly others.

# Grafting

Grafting is the usual means of propagation when growing from seed or cuttings is unreliable. It is often practised with genetic dwarf varieties obtained from natural 'witches' brooms', such as P. sylvestris, vars. Beuvronensis Watereri; Frensham; Dansai (this is my own variety); Andorra etc, and many others. The Japanese use grafting techniques extensively for propagating the cork-bark varieties of pine and many of the *yatsabusa* (many budded) varieties of white pine.

Although there are very many different ways to graft I tend to use the 'whip and tongue' technique for deciduous species and the 'spliced side graft' also known as the 'veneer side graft' for coniferous varieties, especially pines.

There are certain practices that need to be observed if success is to be

▲ *This magnificent specimen of Pinus sylvestris (var. Beuvronensis) is growing in the Pygmy Pinetum, Devizes, England. It is one of the finest varieties of genetic dwarf Scots pine that can be made into Bonsai. It is easy to graft and the union heals over very well.*

▶ *A veneer side graft of Pinus sylvestris (var. Dansai) that has had the stock pruned back leaving vegetative growth only on the scion. It has been planted into a garden rockery to grow on in order to form a mother plant for future propagations.*

achieved. The species used for the root stock and the scion have to be compatible. That is, they should be from the same species and more than that, should display similar characteristics. For instance, two-needle pines will not necessarily unite with three or five-needle varieties but there are exceptions and the five-needled Japanese white pine P. *parviflora var. Pentaphylla* is often grafted on to the two-needled Japanese black pine. I have successfully grafted P. *sylvestris, var. Beuvronensis* on to Japanese black pine. The purpose for this combination is to capitalize on the short-needled characteristics of the Scots pine and the heavy trunk characteristics of the black pine.

Another vital point to remember when grafting is that it is imperative that a portion of the cambium layer of the scion is in contact with the cambium layer of the rootstock. The cambium layer is the circumscribing ring of single cells that is immediately under the outer bark of the tree and appears as a circle of green when looking at the trunk or branch in cross-section. The scion is the name given to the variety of tree that is to be grafted, and the rootstock is the root variety on to which the scion is to be grafted. (It's not as complicated as it sounds!)

The best results are obtained if the scion is dormant and the rootstock is just emerging from dormancy. Therefore, six weeks prior to grafting, bring the rootstocks into a glasshouse to break their dormancy or, conversely, store the scions in a refrigerated place to maintain them in a dormant state until grafting commences. I tend to make my grafts for all species between January and February.

If possible supply bottom heat to the new grafts and keep them in a humid environment such as a wooden frame covered with polythene. The grafts usually take anything up to three months and the swelling of buds and initiation of leaves is a sure sign that the graft has taken. For me, there is nothing more horticulturally satisfying than a successful graft.

Do not be in too much of a hurry to prune back the top growth of the rootstock when veneer side grafting — and when this is actually done, do it in two stages.

Grafts can leave unsightly scars at the point of union so it is best to graft as close to the root crown as possible or use the combined graft and layer technique that I use for crab apples. Although this technique is time consuming it is very effective as not only will you eventually achieve a

low graft, but the rootstock will also produce a good spread of radial roots as a result of the layering technique.

Species that are usually grafted are the coniferous genetic dwarfs on to rootstocks of the same species and a number of the ornamental flowering varieties which will not thrive on their own roots and require rootstocks with greater vigour (species such as red flowering hawthorn, some of the quinces, flowering crab apples etc.) The cork-bark varieties of pine and maple and other similar botanical curiosities are invariably grafted to propagate the cultivar. Incidentally, with crab apples it is best to use one of the vigorous rootstocks such as Apple Seedling rather than one of the dwarfing varieties. This may sound a little cock-eyed but we require vigour in order that the scion will grow well. It will then develop a strong

trunk and be many-branched. These in turn can be pruned back when training commences. If a pedigree dwarfing rootstock such as Malling (M9) is used the scion would be slow to develop and produce too few branches when used for Bonsai purposes. Besides, a vigorous rootstock will also develop a sound root buttress which is a great advantage.

For space reasons I have discussed simple techniques which are most suitable for Bonsai applications but extensive information on the subject of grafting can be found in books such as *The Grafter's Handbook* by R.J.Garner, published by Faber. Grafting is a fascinating process and immensely satisfying when success is achieved. Grafting can also be used to improve rootage and to graft branches onto denuded parts of the tree where additional branches would be desirable.

▲ Whip and tongue grafting Using only dormant scions, cut pencil-thick branches about three inches (75mm) long with two to three buds. Cut a diagonal splice about one inch (25mm) at the base with a reverse splice cut in its centre to form a 'tongue' and do the same on the rootstock which should just be emerging from dormancy. The best time to make grafts is usually in late winter.

Ideally the scion and stock should be as equal in thickness as possible. If there is a mismatch, make sure that the cambium on both scion and stock come into contact at some point or there will be no hope of the graft taking. Press the

scion onto the stock, making sure the tongues interlink, and tie firmly with ribbons of polythene or rubber bands. Try to perform the operation as quickly as possible as the cut ends can soon dry out. Place in a humid environment and provide bottom heat if possible. As soon as signs of growth begin, gradually harden off and remove to a well-ventilated position. Rub off any buds or shoots that grow from the rootstock. The rootstock should be of a similar species to the scion and as closely matched in character as possible. As always, there are exceptions to the rule. For instance, pears are often grafted onto quince stocks.

▼ Veneer side grafting is one of the most popular ways to graft coniferous species, especially pines. Compatibility between scion and rootstock is essential to achieve success. Cut a thin veneer of bark, about one and a half inches (4cm) long on two year-old rootstock as close to the root crown as possible. Cut a similar length splice on the scion with a slightly angled base and place in the mouth. Make sure you do not wet the end. Build up air pressure in the mouth to inhibit the flow of resin until you are ready to place it in position. Make sure that the cambium layer of both scion and

stock are in contact at some point and tie tightly with polythene ribbon or rubber bands. Prune back about a third of the stock and place in a humid environment, supplying bottom heat if possible. As soon as growth begins, harden off and remove to a well-ventilated position. When the shoots are well grown on the scion prune back the rootstock to about two inches (5cm) above the point of union and a year later prune back the remaining snag to form an angled cut. This will produce a neat callous eventually. Grow on in a garden bed to gain size and girth.

► Pinus sylvestris (var. Beuv-ronensis) grafted onto Pinus mugo. This was the very first successful graft I made and in those early days when I had very little access to good material I made the best of a bad job. Note the ugly scar at the point of union. Although mountain pines are notorious for not producing thick trunks, there is a bonus with this combination in that it causes the scion to produce minute needles. To some extent the trunk base can be thickened by gently bruising it with a hammer. This causes the underlying bark cells to swell when they reform, thus giving girth to the trunk. Do not be over-enthusiastic with this technique or you may beat the tree to death!

► The grafted material is planted out into a garden bed for a season to increase the trunk caliper and strengthen the graft union.

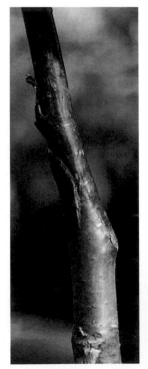

◄ A well-healed graft after one season in the garden bed.

► With a sharp knife remove a ring of bark from all around the rootstock about one and a half inches (4cm) below the point of union. This should be done just after the leaves have hardened off in late spring when there is still plenty of growing season left for photosynthesis to form the necessary sugars and starches etc to make abundant roots. Paint the cut area with a rooting hormone gel or dust with rooting hormone powder.

▲ Whip and tongue graft of flowering crab apple that has had the polythene wrapping removed. After the graft has taken, the technique on right can be applied to improve the root system and reduce the distance between graft union and root crown.

▲ Cut a slit into a five-inch (13cm) diameter plastic pot so that it can be placed around the prepared rootstock and fill it tightly with sphagnum moss impregnated with a vitamin B1 solution such as Superthrive.

▲ This is an example of the ring-barking technique applied to a mountain maple to improve its root spread which was previously one sided.

►Cover the whole of the pot with soil and make sure it does not dry out. Water as necessary over the rest of the growing season but do not allow it to become water-logged. In time a new set of roots will form all around the prepared area. This usually takes a full growing season. Remove the plastic pot and when sufficient roots have developed the original root system can be pruned away, removing the tap root and any other untidy roots. The tree can then be replanted into the garden bed to grow on until the desired size is reached and then potted into a large wooden box for training. Observe normal practice for re-potting. The purpose of this rather long-winded technique is so that one can graft at a convenient height above the roots in the first instance without having to worry too much about grafting close to the root crown, and of course to improve the radial root spread with improved buttress after the ring-barking technique has been applied.

▼ Not only is grafting used as a means of propagation, it is also used to graft branches onto denuded sections of the tree as in the case of this pine. Additional roots can also be grafted onto the base of trees to supplement any deficiencies.

# Propagation from air-layering

Air-layering is a very popular means of propagating plant material and is to be highly recommended for Bonsai. Basically it is a form of cutting that is encouraged to root whilst still attached to the parent plant. It has many advantages, some of which are listed below:

1  It is almost one hundred per cent successful.
2  Mature plant material and thickish branches can easily be encouraged to root.

3  It is ideal in the production of forest style groups as several Potensai can be made from the same clone with an opportunity for generating cuttings of differing thicknesses and identical character.
4  Species that are often difficult to root from cuttings, such as pines, can usually be rooted by air-layering.
5  Newly formed roots can be seen before the plant is severed.
6  Air-layering usually produces an excellent spread of radial roots.

7  In situ training can be commenced before air-layering is applied.
8  It offers a useful way of shortening leggy trunks in Bonsai.
9  It can be used in conjunction with stock that has been grafted to lower the point of union.
10  It is particularly useful for producing twin-trunk, multi-trunk and clump style Bonsai.
11  It is a good way of preparing a new set of radial roots with improved buttress above the original roots which may have several faults.

The two most popular methods of air-layering are the tourniquet and ring-barking techniques. Occasionally, a 'bridge' of bark is left on with the ring-barking method. This is explained in the photo-series on the right.

I use air-layering extensively to produce material for Bonsai as it can be used on such a wide range of trees and shrubs; whether they originate in pots or whether they are garden trees is immaterial. Another bonus the technique has to offer is that the exact length of the trunk can be controlled. This is particularly relevant in the production of broom style zelkova.

▶ *This young mountain maple forest was created from air-layered stock off the same mother tree. It will benefit from the addition of a few more very thin-trunked trees which can easily be made from cuttings or further air-layerings.*

◄ Air-layering is a very simple and effective way of propagating plant material suitable for developing into Bonsai, and the best time to do it is in mid-summer when vegetative growth is most vigorous. The following sequence illustrates the technique very clearly. First, select the material to be layered. In this case it is a grey bark elm grown from a seedling which was transplanted into a garden bed, well fed and watered for a growing season to promote rapid growth. The trunk was strapped to a piece of bamboo cane to make it absolutely straight. At the same time the top of the tree was carefully trained to initiate the broom style.

▲ The clear polythene can be further wrapped with a piece of black polythene to exclude light and absorb more heat. Air-layers can be top heavy so use an additional stake to stabilize the tree.

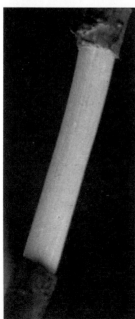

◄ A ring of bark about one and a quarter inches (3cm) long was removed approximately ten inches (25cm) below the first branch. (With thicker trunks, it is advisable to leave a one eighths of an inch (3mm) 'bridge' of bark rather than to encircle the tree completely. This will serve as a lifeline. Now paint the cut area with a rooting hormone gel (or dust with rooting hormone powder) and cover with ample sphagnum moss impregnated with a vitamin B1 solution such as Superthrive. Wrap the moss over with a clear polythene sheet and tie tightly with plastic string that will not rot.

◄ Remove the black polythene from time to time to check for developing roots and if it is necessary to water the layer, do so with the aid of a syringe. **Never** let an air-layer dry out.

▲ When sufficient roots have formed, the layered section can be cut away from the parent plant provided it is not during the winter season (unless adequate protection from frost can be supplied). I prefer to wrap an 'overcoat' of glass-fibre roofing insulation matting around the whole of the layer and wait until the following spring before severing the tree. After the tree has been severed, remove the polythene wrapping and very carefully tease out the sphagnum moss with a chopstick. It will be found that the new roots are extremely brittle at this stage and will snap easily. Spray with fresh water periodically to prevent the roots from drying out. Notice the absence of a tap root and how well spread the roots are around the base of the trunk. Incidentally the original trunk can be encouraged to sprout and more layers can be made at a later date. The process can go on almost indefinitely. Plant the layer in a large wooden box and treat it as a king-size cutting for a year or two. Make sure it has been tied down firmly; position away from the wind. ▼

▲ This trident maple is being air-layered and has had all of its branches removed from one side so that it can be trained into a raft style Bonsai.

▲ The same tree cut away from its parent plant and planted into a large wooden box to await future training.

◄ Another useful way of creating broom style grey-bark elms is to prune the top out of a suitably straight trained tree to form an asymmetric 'V' using a junior hacksaw.

► Tidy up the sawn end with a sharp knife.

◄ Wrap some wet sphagnum moss loosely around the cut area to prevent it drying out and hold it in place with plastic mesh.

► Place a couple of wire arches over the trunk and stretch a polythene bag over it to create a humid environment.

▲ This technique can be very successfully applied to field-grown stock.

▲ Prune out all but two of the new shoots.

◄ Wrap some split garden hose-pipe around the top to reduce clumsy swellings as the new shoots develop and, when they reach a sufficient thickness, prune them back in turn to slightly staggered heights to encourage further shoots to develop. Once again, prune these back to two shoots to create a mathematical progression of one, two, four, eight branches etc. Remove the pieces of hose as soon as primary branches have reached the desired thickness.

▲ After a few weeks several shoots will form around the top of the tree and the wrappings can be removed.

◄ Here is a tree in a garden bed that has had the above technique applied to it. It is now ready to have its secondary branches pruned back to two each per primary branch. In time it will be air-layered to form a new set of roots and potted into a box so that refined training can commence. This explains why broom style zelkova are amongst the most expensive of all Bonsai. As extreme as this technique may appear, it is well worth the trouble for the results it ultimately produces are splendid.

# Pests and diseases

*Leafy meal consumed*
*a Bonsai remains unshown*
*fly by butterfly*

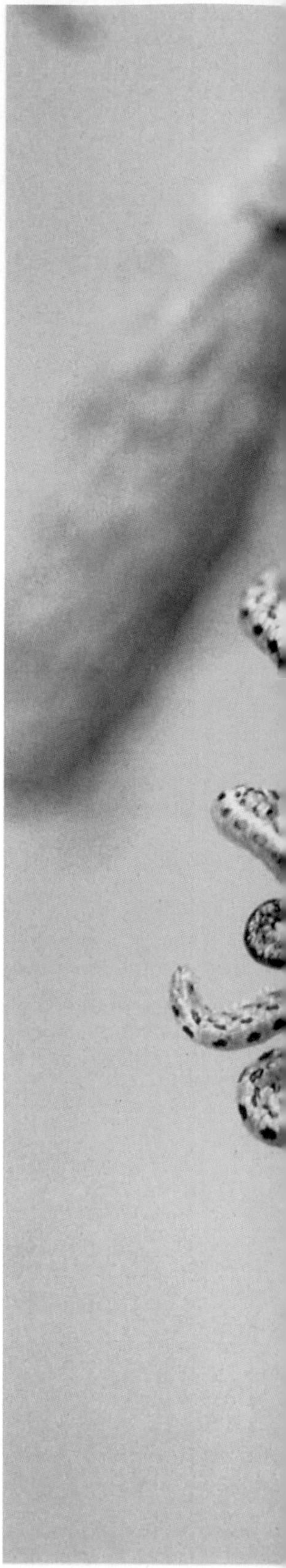

Bonsai are just as susceptible to pests and diseases as their full-grown counterparts in nature and although the range of damage is extensive, by taking simple precautions most can be eliminated.

To deal specifically with every possible pest and disease would fill several volumes as varieties differ according to country and locality so I shall concentrate here on precautionary practice rather than cure. Some treatments for damaged or diseased trees will be included but with sensible forethought most potential pests and diseases can be avoided.

Most countries will have specialist firms that cater for their local conditions and these firms will usually supply free and comprehensive lists of the pesticides, fungicides and herbicides that they manufacture to control the various problems. Enquire at your local garden centre for details and addresses of such companies and write to them for particulars. In cases where a diagnosis cannot be certain write to the governing ministry of agriculture or equivalent in your country giving details of the problem and you will usually find them most helpful. Of course your local Bonsai society may also prove helpful.

Pests and diseases invariably fall into the category of physical, chemical or biological:

## Physical hazards

Physical danger to Bonsai usually results from bad siting. Excessive exposure to extreme sun can have a scorching effect on the plant. This problem is compounded if the tree has been watered in this state. The residual beadlets of water will act as magnifying glasses and cause localized burning on leaves and flowers. Insufficient sunlight will result in leggy growth of vegetative material deficient in chlorophyll, lacking in vigour and anaemic in appearance. Severe winds will also cause scorching of leaves which will become brown around the edges. Wind can also result in the trees being blown over or out of their pots with disastrous consequences.

Ill-considered siting may also subject Bonsai to frost and dehydration from frozen conditions. Usually it is the root end of the tree that is most susceptible to frost damage, so obviously adequate protection must be provided. A cold greenhouse, garden shed with ample light, improvised housing from polythene or placing in a protected part of the garden will usually suffice when frost is anticipated. Do not mollycoddle trees, however, by bringing them indoors to a centrally-heated room. This is likely to do just as much harm.

Physical damage can also be sustained if trees are situated where pet dogs can urinate on them or even knock them over. Protect from all pets. I once found our tortoise happily chewing away at one of my trees! Protect too, from clumsy humans — there are many of them — particularly over-enthusiastic friends who in their eagerness to admire a particular specimen can knock over everything in sight. Obviously the remedy for any of these conditions is to be aware of them in the first place and to consider carefully the best situation in the garden which will prevent the problem arising.

## Chemical hazards

Chemical disorders usually result from poor composts, mineral deficiencies or excessive fertilizing, waterlogging or drought conditions and unsuitable Ph levels.

It is important to make sure that nutritionally imbalanced composts are correctly mixed with the right chemical additives to begin with. (See the section on composts on page 28.) Any chemical excess or deficiency in the compost is likely to result in all sorts of symptoms which usually manifest themselves in the leaves of the plant and which are not always easy to diagnose. It is vital to pay attention to the preparation of composts and to make sure regular fertilizing is carried out in respect of each species and in respect of the age of the tree. (See the section on fertilizing on page 36.)

Most problems from this source are usually created by overfeeding which can cause root scorching and/or osmosis, resulting in the denial of liquids to the plant in spite of ample water being supplied. If in any doubt, underfeed rather than overfeed. It is much easier to nurse a tree back to health that is suffering from nutritional starvation than the other way round. Again it is a question of being alert to this type of damage and making sure that a regular and sensible fertilizing regime is maintained.

Incidentally overfeeding can also result in unsightly slime moulds forming on the surface of pots.

Most chemical disorders appear in discolouration of the leaves and when the diagnosis has been established treatment should be applied in the form of a nutritional supplement. For instance, nitrogen deficiency is witnessed in stunted growth and pale yellowy, sometimes red leaves. Leaves scorched at their edges are likely to be deficient in potash whilst a deficiency in magnesium is usually displayed as a brownish colour between the leaf veins. Yellow between the leaf veins can usually be attributed to shortage of iron. An application of an appropriate foliar feed will usually redress the situation with regard to nitrogen and potash deficiencies whilst watering with a sequestrated compound will supplement the iron/magnesium deficiency.

Waterlogged composts that result from pots with poor drainage facilities are probably responsible for more Bonsai deaths than any other cause. It is essential to use a well-draining compost and to provide adequate drainage holes in the base of pots. This is often a difficult situation to detect until it is too late but trees that are suffering from stagnant water will obviously be growing in soil that looks wet and has an unpleasant, sour 'boggy' smell. The tree is reluctant to put out forward growth, lacks vigour and usually looks somewhat insipid in colour; branches die off inexplicably and eventually the tree dies. If waterlogging is suspected, remove the tree from the pot and examine the roots. Healthy young roots will be bright and amber to creamy-white in colour and somewhat brittle with a pleasant, earthy smell. Diseased roots will be black and mostly hollow with rotten centres. They will mush easily when squeezed between the fingers and tend to have a sour or bad eggs' smell. If this is the case, prune back the diseased roots until sound ones, if any, are reached and re-pot in a suitable compost; place in a humid environment and treat as

a king-sized cutting. Do not water any more than is necessary to maintain the compost at a comfortably damp state and keep your fingers tightly crossed!

Underwatering and consequent drought will result in limp green shoots and foliage in the plant, and, at an advanced stage, in dried curly leaves that remain on the tree. Provided the condition has been short-lived, a possible remedy is to water the tree and spray the foliage frequently. It should also be placed in a shady position out of the wind. Once again, provide humidity and do not overwater.

pH refers to the levels of alkalinity and aciditity in the soil; whereas most plants are able to encompass a wide tolerance of these levels there are some that must be planted in acid soils to thrive. Azaleas, rhododendrons and other ericaceous species fall into this category. Too much lime in the compost inhibits the uptake of iron and manganese. If this is the case, add plenty of peat and leaf mould to the compost and water once a year with a sequestrated compound. If possible use rain water in preference to tap water particularly if the local water supply tends to be 'hard'.

Whatever problems are caused by chemical deficiencies do remember that the Bonsai in a sense is a captive tree that cannot escape from its container environment, so redress any chemical deficiencies very sparingly and very gradually. Many well-intentioned Bonsai enthusiasts kill off their trees by grossly over-fertilizing or by exceeding manufacturers' recommended dilutions. Moderation is essential in the application of any chemicals to Bonsai and whenever possible their use as a cure should be avoided by creating the right conditions in the first place.

## Biological hazards

The biological type of threat is the most extensive to confront Bonsai. The following diseases or infections are responsible: weeds, bacteria and viruses, fungi, insects and pests.

## Weeds

These are the simplest to control. In a pot situation weeds are usually introduced by using loams in the compost that have been taken from the surface strata of soil where weed seeds are prevalent. Seeds are also blown in by the wind from innumerable sources and are found in bird droppings. Whatever their source, weeds remain a

nuisance, upsetting the visual balance of the Bonsai and also consuming nutrients intended for the tree. Remove them with pincers as soon as they appear.

In garden beds where Potensai have been planted out to increase their size weeds may

occur in such quantities you may have to resort to the use of herbicides. If this is the case, make sure you use herbicides that destroy weeds through the leaves and avoid the soil-drenching varieties. These latter types will invariably spread to the roots of the Potensai killing them too. Apply

appropriate herbicide by selective spraying on to weeds on wind-free days.

If weeds are growing too close to Potensai to use sprays effectively, it will be necessary to use a dutch hoe or hand fork. When weeds are removed in this way, take care not to distribute their seeds further or the problem will be compounded.

## Bacteria and viruses

Bacteria and viruses account for many tree diseases which are still proving scientifically difficult to control. If it is

confirmed that a tree disease is directly attributable to one of these causes it is best to

burn the tree to prevent further spread of the disease and to sterilize the pot and any tools that

may have come into contact with the tree. Do not use the infected compost for any other Bonsai.

## Fungi

Fungi and insect infections probably account for the majority of tree diseases and every part of the tree can be vulnerable to attack but, as mentioned earlier, if certain precautions are

taken the problem can be greatly reduced.

Fungal infection can be minimized if composts are carefully prepared and

comply with the recommendations made earlier (see page 32). Furthermore, routine spraying with a dilute fungicide, preferably of

the systemic variety, once a month will also help to keep trees free of disease. Avoid excessive watering and over-fertilizing which will aggravate the problem and keep the trees well ventilated. Deciduous trees are more prone to fungal infections than coniferous.

Should a tree show signs of fungal infection try spraying it once a week for four to five weeks with a weak solution of systemic fungicide alternating with a liquid copper fungicide.

The problem with fungicides is that they will also destroy the beneficial fungi such as the Mycorrhiza fungi so necessary for healthy roots in pines, oaks and other species. So after treating the infected trees, allow a few weeks to pass and add some fresh mycelia from healthy trees to the treated compost to regenerate the symbiotic relationship between roots and Mycorrhiza fungi. Mycelium moulds can look quite alarming when first encountered in a tree's root system and the initial reaction is to think that the plant is diseased. Its presence in a tree's roots is usually indicative of a healthy

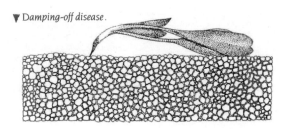

▼ *Damping-off disease.*

state so do not remove it or treat with a fungicide. Roots containing Mycorrhiza have a distinctive pungent fungal smell. Do not confuse root fungi with infestations of root aphids which can look very similar at a first glance.

Some of the moulds, mildews and rots that are attributable to fungal infections most common in Bonsai culture are: damping-off; Verticillium wilt (mostly associated with acers); grey mould (Botrytis); peach leaf curl; powdery mildew and rust. Most of these infections can be eliminated if routine sprayings with systemic fungicides

(containing Benomyl), alternated with liquid copper fungicides are applied as described above.

Damping-off disease affects seedlings causing rot to occur at the base of the plant so that they fall over. Treat with Cheshunt Compound.

Verticillium wilt attacks the sapwood in maples causing rapid die-back of affected branches or trunk. It can be seen as longitudinal blackish striations in the sapwood if an infected part is spliced along its length. It is a difficult condition to cure; treat with systemic fungicide containing

Benomyl by drenching soil around the base of the plant. Remove the infected sections and burn them.

Grey mould (Botrytis) usually occurs on flowers and leaves situated in high humidity with poor ventilation. Treat it with systemic fungicide containing Benomyl.

Peach leaf curl occurs on several of the prunus species and appears as large reddish blisters on the leaves which absciss (separate from the tree) prematurely. Treat this with a copper oxychloride based fungicide.

Powdery mildew appears as a white mealy growth on leaf surfaces and should be treated with systemic fungicide containing Benomyl.

Rust appears as brown or yellow raised spots on leaves. Remove the infected leaves and burn and if necessary spray with a fungicide containing Zineb.

## Insects and pests

Although Bonsai are vulnerable to infections from most of the plant-attacking insects and pests it is only a small number that proves persistently troublesome. As ever prevention is better than cure so precautionary sprayings with dilute insecticides makes good sense. The

types of insecticides used should be rotated to cater for insect-contact, leaf-contact and systemic function. Winter sprays of tar oil-based insecticides applied in mid-winter are also a good practice as these asphyxiate winter-hibernating 'bugs' and their eggs. Avoid

spraying insecticides onto newly opened leaves as they can be seriously damaged by the chemicals and their growth inhibited. In cases where virgin leaves have been attacked, particularly by greenfly, it is better to wash the offenders off with a gentle hosing of water and after

the leaves have hardened two to three weeks later, to spray as normal.

I find the best way to eradicate insect and pest infestations is to apply routine sprays of appropriate insecticides or pesticides on a weekly basis for four to five weeks irrespective of the type of

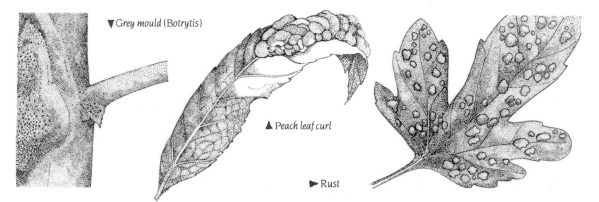

▼ *Grey mould (Botrytis)*

▲ *Peach leaf curl*

▶ *Rust*

insect. Single sprayings usually result in the speedy return of the offenders after the initial punishment.

Insects of different types will attack roots, trunk, branches, leaves, flowers and fruit causing diverse problems. When applying insecticides a helpful tip is to add two to three drops of washing-up liquid to the insecticide to facilitate penetration of the insects' waxy coating. Mealy bugs and woolly aphids can be destroyed more easily with this technique. Large insects such as caterpillars can be physically removed and destroyed and scale insects are best killed by painting with a suitable brush dipped in methylated spirits. The winter tar-oil sprays are also particularly effective against these insects.

Innumerable insecticides have been developed, and reference to a selection of manufacturers' catalogues and trade lists is to be recommended in order to find a suitable insecticide for a specific infection.

## Soil-based insects and pests

Cutworms are soil-living caterpillars that may be brown, grey or green and can grow up to two inches (5cm). They damage roots and seedling stems, often eating their way right through.

Chafer grubs are the larval stage of the may-bug or cockchafer and are plump white curved grubs about one inch (25mm) long that feed on plant roots.

Vine weevils are similar to chafer grubs but smaller. They too feed on plant roots.

Root aphids are mouldy grey creatures similar to blackfly that live in colonies amongst the roots of trees, particularly pines. They suck nourishment from the tree roots and can easily be mistaken for beneficial Mycorrhizal fungus.

Leatherjackets are tough-skinned grey-brown larvae of the cranefly. They feed on roots and sometimes birds peck the moss surface dressing off Bonsai pots to get at the leatherjackets underneath.

Treat all the above pests by asking for the specific pesticide at your local garden centre. These will usually contain active ingredients such as Aldrin, Fenitrothion or Oxamyl.

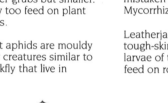

▲ Cutworm

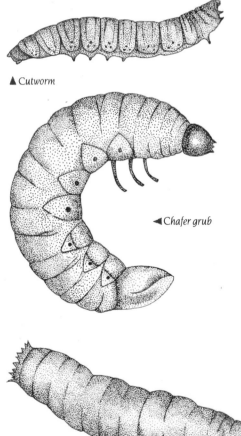

◄ Chafer grub

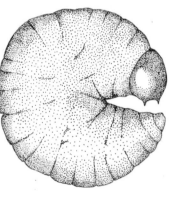

◄ Vine weevil grub

▼ The creamy-yellow mould on the plastic mesh in the centre of the picture is Mycorrhiza fungi, a beneficial fungus that forms a symbiotic relationship with the roots of the tree, in this case a Scots pine. The greyish-white mould around the rest of the roots is an infestation of root aphids.

▲ Leatherjacket

## Trunk, branch and bark insects and pests

These can belong to the group of borers, suckers, cankers or gall-forming infections. Bonsai in England are generally free of most of these pests with the exception of scale insects which appear as tiny limpet-shell like creatures that tend to remain in the same spot on the bark of trees and which sometimes form a white fluffy under mattress. They suck

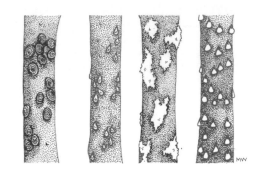

nourishment from the bark and can increase to alarming numbers. Treat by spraying with a tar-oil spray in winter or wipe off manually with a brush dipped in methylated spirits.

◄ *Scale*

▼ *Newly propagated stock and accent plantings may be vulnerable if there are snails in the vicinity.*

## Leaf pests and insects

Probably the most vulnerable part of any Bonsai to attacks from pests or diseases is in the leafy regions of the tree. Although possible dangers from this source can be extensive, in practice only a few 'bugs' tend to prove persistently troublesome. Here is a list of the more commonly encountered ones:

Caterpillars will eat the leaves of the Bonsai and often distort them by attaching several leaves together with sticky webs. Remove these where possible and destroy them, then spray the tree with an insecticide containing malathion as a precaution against any caterpillars that might be hidden from sight.

Leaf miner can be identified by the long winding tunnels which have been eaten into the tissue of the leaves by the small grubs. Spray with malathion.

Slugs and snails are more harmful to newly propagated stock and the leaves of certain accent plantings than to the Bonsai. Scatter slug pellets on the soil around infected trees to poison the offenders.

Greenfly and blackfly are amongst the most common foliage pests and should be sprayed with malathion to control. They are often preyed upon by ladybirds which are harmless and should therefore be encouraged.

Capsid-bug damage manifests itself in the leaves at first by causing reddish-brown spots to appear. As the leaf expands these spots will tear to produce holes with ragged brown edges. Spray with an insecticide containing Fenitrothion.

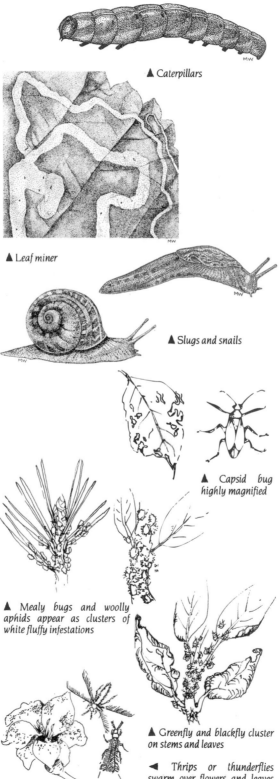

▲ Caterpillars

▲ Leaf miner

▲ Slugs and snails

▲ Capsid bug highly magnified

▲ Mealy bugs and woolly aphids appear as clusters of white fluffy infestations

▲ Greenfly and blackfly cluster on stems and leaves

◄ Thrips or thunderflies swarm over flowers and leaves

Red spider mite is virtually invisible to the naked eye but it can be detected by a faint mottling on the upper surface of the leaves. Examination of the lower side of the leaf with a powerful magnifying glass will confirm the presence of the mites. Red spider mite is difficult to eradicate. Spray with systemic liquid insecticide, or malathion. Do not use systemic insecticides on Chinese elms as this can cause the leaves to absciss (drop).

Woolly aphids and mealy bugs are very similar at first glance. Both appear as infestations of a white downy cluster usually around the young shoots of the trees and are particularly prevalent in pines. Spray regularly with an insecticide containing malathion and add a few drops of washing up liquid to make the pests' waxy covering easier to penetrate.

Thrips or thunderflies can be a problem during hot weather. They tend to swarm over the leaves and flowers and appear as a silvery flecking. Spray with malathion.

When spraying any chemicals onto Bonsai, avoid breathing in any of the spray and if possible wear a nose mask. Most insecticides, fungicides and herbicides are toxic and can cause serious problems to health so always keep them well out of the reach of children. As a general guide never exceed the recommended dilution rate for any pesticides used in the control of weeds, fungi, insects and pests. Avoid spraying infected plants in wet, damp, windy or extremely sunny conditions.

Line illustrations on pages 96-99 by Melanie Williams

# Case histories

*Chattering crickets*
*bouncing ball and crashing dog*
*silent summer breeze*

In this chapter I will be discussing the origins and design history of some of my trees. It will soon become apparent that Bonsai is a continually changing art-form and that no tree is ever finished in the absolute sense. Ideas relating to style and form can be altered at almost any point in a tree's life. This of course is what makes the art so exciting. It is never static and the results are mutually rewarding. The Bonsai benefits and thrives from the care, attention and love lavished on it and responds by providing

endless pleasure and satisfaction for its designer. It is almost like a love affair and a relationship between owner and tree invariably develops. It is art with a 'fourth dimension'. That is, the dimension of life; sacred and worthy of contemplation and, when the Bonsai is in its most elevated state, of edification.

Also included in this chapter are a number of 'before' and 'after' photographs of trees designed by students attending my Bonsai

workshops. Attending a workshop on Bonsai design is one of the quickest ways of mastering the various techniques and enthusiasts should search out experienced Bonsai designers and dealers who provide courses and workshop facilities. More and more are becoming available with the increase in Bonsai expertise in the Western hemisphere. It also makes sense to attend workshops conducted by different teachers as every individual tends to have a slightly different approach to the subject which can

broaden your experience.

The trees that I have selected for this section cover a variety of species and styles and have originated from many different sources. They are not arranged in any particular order. Most of the examples included still need to be refined further and, apart from the literati Scots pine, none is as yet mature, so a lot of natural changes such as the production of mature bark have yet to occur. I have great expectations of these trees and much to look forward to.

## Wellingtonia *Sequoiadendron giganteum*

I first thought this tree was a *Cryptomeria japonica* when I purchased it from a garden centre in Exeter in November 1977 and I estimated its age at the time to be about seven years old. Its trunk at the root crown was just over an inch (25mm) in diameter and in those days I considered this to be big. Very little information was available at the time on sequoias as Bonsai, so this provided a good opportunity to do some pioneering work with the species.

I kept the tree in its bag pot for a couple of seasons making sure it was abundantly watered and fertilized and it responded well to this treatment. This species appreciates plenty of water and likes to have its foliage sprayed frequently. I noticed it had the habit of shedding a fairly high percentage of its foliage each autumn. And although trees of this species appear to be entirely hardy when planted out in garden beds, when they are in a pot environment I prefer to provide protection from frost by placing them in a cold greenhouse during the winter. I think this facilitates rejuvenation of

NOV 77

new shoots the following spring. If too much foliage is shed in any given autumn it is better to keep the tree in a greenhouse until late spring of the following year when the new shoots are advanced in their development. Then the tree can be introduced to the display bench once it has been hardened off.

In training this particular tree, I concentrated first on making sure the trunk was straight. I then slit the undersides of the branches with a penknife to about three inches

▲ *A container-grown Welling-tonia purchased from a garden centre in Exeter in 1977. I was not 100 per cent sure what to do with this tree so it remained in the bag pot for a season or two where it was pruned back hard and fer-tilized and watered well. I also initiated the structuring and wiring of the branches whilst it was still in this pot.*

(75mm) from the point where they joined the trunk. This was done so that the callousing scar would improve the 'holding' capacity after the branches had been

wire-trained. Otherwise there would be a tendency for the branches to rise back to their original positions. The technique worked very well.

When I finally got round to potting up the Potensai, I was amazed at the size and quantity of the roots. These were carefully untangled and about two-thirds of them pruned away and the cut ends treated with a wound sealant. To compliment the height of the tree and its austere upright style it was planted in a relatively shallow pot but as the species prefers to have a rich compost and some depth to the soil, I decided to mound up the soil in order to satisfy the horticultural as well as the aesthetic needs. The tree is also well fertilized each year.

During the growing season the foliage is continually finger pinched to encourage finer and tighter shoots. All downward pointing shoots are removed as soon as they appear in order to emphasize the curved undulations of the upper foliage clouds. Observation of mature specimens in our parks confirms that the tips of

▲ The tree was transplanted into its next pot in the spring of 1980 after it had been extensively root-pruned. In order to rebuild a fibrous root system I used a large, deep pot with a rich compost containing a fair amount of loam.

▲ There was a nasty bend in the trunk of the tree, so I applied a heavy duty clamp for about one year to correct it. It has made some difference but there is still a slight lean towards the back of the tree. One cannot apply too much pressure with this species as its bark is very thick and soft and the clamp might tend to bite into it.

▲ In 1984 the tree was re-potted into a shallow pot with scalloped corners and the compost mounded up slightly to maintain depth. It was allowed to grow on unchecked to encourage the production of shoots so that I could build up the foliage pads.

▲ By 1985 the new growth has been reduced by finger pinching to shape the foliage into more rounded forms and at the same time to introduce better defined spaces between the branches. A photograph of this tree was sent to the International Bonsai and Suiseki Exhibition, in Osaka, Japan where it won a certificate of merit.

the branches often tend to curve upwards resembling miniature trees growing at the ends of each branch.

For the time being I shall maintain a rounded crown at the top of the tree but the sketches show some possible variations in style that I am applying to some other sequoias in training.

What is so nice about this species is that it is easy to train and can become a very convincing reflection of its natural counterpart in a relatively short space of time. Incidentally Potensai of this species respond well to planting out in a garden bed for three to four years where they will increase in girth at an amazing rate.

Once the Bonsai is well established in its pot allow three to five years between re-potting sessions. I can strongly recommend this species for Bonsai.

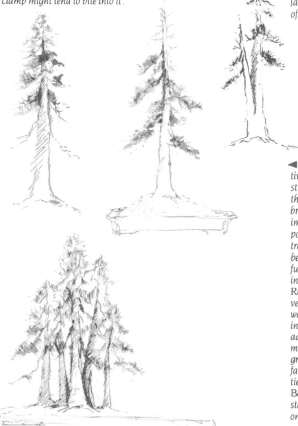

◀ The four sketches show alternative variations in the future styling of this tree. I could jin out the top or jin out some of the lower branches which would give the impression of great age. Another possibility would be to change the tree into a split-trunk style, but before this could be done successfully the tree would need to increase considerably in girth. Remember that this species has very thick bark and ample sapwood is required before attempting a split-trunk style. By adding some more trees I could make a very attractive forest group on the lines of John Naka's famous 'Goshin'. The possibilities are enormous, which is why Bonsai is so exciting — it is never static, and can be as varied as one's imagination.

## Blackthorn or sloe
### *Prunus spinosa*

I collected this tree from the side of a footpath in Gloucestershire. It had obviously been trodden on frequently by passers-by and was damaged. I potted it up in a seed tray where it remained for several years as I was not sure how to style it. It was later transplanted into a tiny stoneware pot, and eventually in November 1977 I decided to train it in the rock-grown style.

The tree was pruned back and planted in a shallow hole, not much larger than a thimble, on an attractive piece of rock I found in south Devon and has remained there ever since.

Each November it is fertilized with bonemeal and every spring it rewards me with a beautiful display of

flowers and occasionally fruit. It has had a minimum of formal training and I am quite content to retain it as an untrained specimen — warts and all!

The early display of flowers each year is a welcome reminder that winter has passed and warm and extended days will soon be back. I find this annual experience sublimely comforting and, if for no other reason than this, every Bonsai enthusiast should have at least one sloe in his collection. This species does not enjoy the popularity it deserves. It is incredibly hardy and can be adapted to many styles — including a number of the more dramatic forms such as split-trunk, hollow-trunk, driftwood, literati etc.

▲ *A blackthorn collected in 1973 about ten to fifteen years old. The tree was planted in a seed tray where it remained for a few years.*

NOV 77

▲ *In autumn 1977 I transplanted the tree onto this piece of rock having first pruned off a number of branches and roots. With hindsight perhaps I should have left the long branch on the right as it tended to give movement and direction to the tree. I am now in the process of re-growing this branch. It is perhaps fortuitous that in those early days I was uncertain about how to style the tree as I now find it very satisfying in this somewhat natural presentation. I could so easily have obeyed 'the rules' and straight-jacketed the tree into something entirely contrived which of course would have been far less rewarding.*

◀ *To enhance the natural image further, in 1984 I planted some Arenaria balearica as an underplanting. This tree has now been on this piece of rock for over nine years without a change of soil. Each November it is fertilized with bonemeal. Perhaps in a year or two I may scratch away some of the soil and replace it with some fresh but for the time being it will remain as it is and also remain one of my favourite Bonsai. The tree is given winter protection each year by being placed in a cold greenhouse.*

# Scots pine *Pinus sylvestris var.* Watereri

This was created from container-grown grafted stock purchased from a garden centre in 1972. It is a somewhat leggy tree, lacking a back branch.

I decided to style this tree as a formal upright Bonsai, not appreciating in those early days how difficult a task this would be using a Potensai with such a paucity of branches. But there were so few books on Bonsai then and seemingly no one around who shared the interest, so I was virtually on my own. I persevered anyway but from the start it has been an exercise in trying to make a silk purse out of a sow's ear. The main reason for this is because the species is fastigiate in habit. That is, its branches have a tendency to grow upwards and are therefore very difficult to train. The branches also tend to become disproportionately thick when compared to the trunk, especially in the upper part of the tree. The whole exercise has been a nightmare and I would not recommend this species to anyone for Bonsai unless they have masochistic tendencies! There are many other varieties of genetic dwarf Scots pine much more suitable for Bonsai treatment.

To thicken the root stock I have used the bark hammering technique which is displaying positive results.

*▶ 1986. The tree has been re-potted into an Indian red stoneware pot of fairly formal character to compliment its own form. I still have to improve the buttress at the base of the trunk and to rewire and reposition every single twig to improve the silhouette and lower the foliage pads. When this is complete I might be persuaded to like the tree, but fourteen years of training is a very long time to have only reached this far. Is a 'silk purse' possible!?*

*◀ This ridiculous little grafted Scots pine, var. Watereri was purchased from a local garden centre in 1972. It has been a nightmare for me ever since and I shall never know why I bother to keep it. Someone once said to me that Bonsai is all about love/hate relationships and I am still trying to find some love so far as this tree is concerned!*

*▶ In 1978 the tree was re-potted into an oversized pot in order to encourage growth and vigour and the branches were wired in a vain attempt to create a formal upright style.*

*◀ The tree had been well fertilized and by 1979 the new candles were allowed to extend to strengthen the roots and thicken the trunk. In mid-August they will be pruned back to two or three pairs of needles. This will encourage the production of buds. The tree lacks depth as it has no back branch so I will try to overcome this by growing a branch from the back of the bottom right branch and when it is long enough train it around to the back of the tree.*

*▲ By 1980 at last the tree is showing some promise but the trunk is still too thin and the graft union rather ugly. Unfortunately this variety will not grow well on its own roots and needs to be grafted, or I would have considered air-layering it to eliminate the graft union and at the same time reduce the legginess of the tree. The bottom left-hand branch is developing well and has formed quite an acceptable foliage cloud but a lot of work still needs to be done on the rest of the tree. I have resorted to the hammering technique to thicken the lower trunk and it is responding slowly. I originally tried slashing the bark at the back of the trunk with a penknife to facilitate trunk swelling. This did have some effect but tended to leave very unsightly scars which caused the bark to grow in an uncharacteristic manner.*

## Scots pine *Pinus sylvestris var. Beuvronensis*

'Big Matsu', as this tree is fondly called, (matsu being Japanese for pine) originated from nursery stock purchased in 1974. I estimated its age at the time to be around eight years old. Most of my affection for and knowledge of pines has come from my association with this tree. Because I owe it a great deal and although it has in its structure many classical faults, it will always have a very special place in my collection.

What is so interesting is that although its faults are classical (spokewheel branches, bar branches etc), it nevertheless works well aesthetically.

The tree has been designed in the informal upright style and the photographs illustrate the structural changes made during its early years in training. Note how the original inverted triangle has been totally reversed. Although this tree has been grafted there is no visible evidence of the union; it has healed over remarkably well. The surface root spread is a little one-sided so I have cheated by placing a piece of wood bark on the other side to simulate roots which has worked amazingly well. It has been in place for about eight years and no one appears to have noticed any difference!

▲ If the Watereri Scots pine proved a nightmare to train, this tree has been a dream. I purchased it from an exhibitor of dwarf conifers at a local flower show in 1974. It was at the time the biggest tree in my collection and was my introduction to trees of a more challenging nature.

▲ In 1975 my first task was to lower the bottom right-hand branch. This was done by making a suitable template out of mild steel lined with thick felt to protect the bark on the branch. It was then 'G' cramped onto the branch and gradually coaxed into position by tightening the cramps over a period of months. This view is from the rear of the tree.

▲ A year later the cramp has been removed and the branch is in its new position. The trunk has also had some wire-training but, with this particular variety of Scots pine, any branches over three quarters of an inch (2cm) thick tend to be extremely difficult to bend. Note the wiring scars on the trunk. It will take six to eight years to recover from these scars but they will in time disappear. The tree has been re-potted into a stoneware pot which is totally unsuitable but at the time I knew no better.

▲ 1978. The tree has been re-potted into a much larger stoneware pot to encourage growth and vigour. I have pruned out the branch growing between the first branch and the trunk. This has left rather a large space so the crown will have to be trained down to reduce the gap. Note that a cramp has been temporarily replaced on the lower right-hand branch as the branch has started to rise back up. I also slit the bark underneath the branch to create a healing callous that would cause the branch to hold its position better.

▲ Having allowed the tree to grow unchecked in 1978, in 1979 it had its first real refinement training to establish the peripheral outlines and relate the main foliage masses. Note the fungi growing by the trunk. This is always a sign of good health in pines and indicative of a prolific root system.

▲ 1981. Further refinement training has been applied to the tree and the twig 'knuckles' under the foliage pads are beginning to show. The pot is too big for the tree and is too severe for the style but it has served well for training purposes.

▲ The tree has been extensively thinned out to give the foliage some breathing space and now in 1983 it is being allowed to grow on again to encourage prolific bud production. The new growth will be pruned back to two to three pairs of needles per shoot in late summer. Meanwhile it will be watered and fertilized very sparingly so as to keep the needle length down to a minimum.

▲ 1986. I am not happy with this pot and have commissioned a new design for the tree in a reddish-black clay _body_. I also need to widen the left-hand side of the upper foliage crown very slightly to improve the overall balance and harmony of the tree. So far it has taken only twelve years to transform Potensai to Bonsai.

◄ Although I am very happy with `Big Matsu' the way it is, here are two other possibilities I have considered for the future. Note too, the shape of the pot.

▲ Two-year old Chinese juniper cutting photographed in 1972.

# Chinese juniper
## *Juniperus Chinensis var. x blaauw*

This tree originated from a cutting made in 1970 and has been designed in the root-over-rock style. The photographs show the technique I used to initiate the design which is a good method for training any species over rock. I am quite pleased with the progress this tree has made and am now continuing the process of refining the foliage. This will involve rigorous finger pinching of the foliage throughout each growing season and making sure the contours and undulations of the foliage define the main branch structures and at the same time relate to each other so as to maintain a form texturally homogeneous.

It will still require many years of training before there is any substantial increase in the girth of the trunk as the species is very slow in growing. It is important to remove all of the downward-pointing growth to expose the underlying 'finger' branches that support the foliage clouds. By adopting this technique you can create a delightfully sparkling filigree of pattern, not unlike that of a stained-glass window.

◄ The cutting was removed from its pot and the soil washed off the roots. It then had its roots spread and tied over a piece of rock and was planted in a plastic bag pot. In 1973 I cut a thin slither of plastic from around the top of the pot to expose the soil and facilitate its erosion.

◄ 1974. The trimming of the plastic pot continued, thus exposing more soil to the erosion process until the roots of the tree began to appear.

◄ In 1976 when sufficient root had been exposed, the rest of the bag pot was removed and the tree transplanted into a fairly deep training pot. Note how the foliage has been allowed to grow on unchecked.

► In 1980 the tree was re-potted once more, this time into a shallower pot. No foliage has been pruned as this vegetative growth will help promote the thickening of the trunk.

NOV 80

▲ By 1986 I felt there had been sufficient growth and the tree was pruned and wire trained. The foliage clouds had been pinched continually to help them inter-relate and to create a series of undulating contours. I am very pleased with the progress this tree has made and it clearly demonstrates that fairly convincing results can be achieved from very humble beginnings. I shall continue to pinch the new growth to improve the overall shape. The tree has been re-potted into an oval 'yamaki' pot.

## Japanese mountain maple
### *Acer palmatum*

When I purchased this Bonsai way back in 1973, I was 'over the moon'. It was a genuine imported tree from Japan and I was ecstatic. What bliss there is in ignorance!

The pot in which it was growing was barely four inches (10cm) in diameter and all the branches grew straight up. It had not really been trained in any way but in those halcyon years, who cared? Well

after a short time I soon realised that I did. Training of the tree commenced and now as I look back in hindsight I realise that this little fellow was probably my most challenging project. It certainly proved to be the most stubborn, unwilling to comply with the structure I had in mind for it; although this was nothing particularly special — just a simple little informal upright style.

◀ I purchased this imported Japanese mountain maple from a local garden centre in 1973. The diameter of the pot was barely four inches (10cm).

▲ Summer 1986. The tree has been re-potted into an oval pot with a very attractive crazed glaze (made by Gordon Duffett).

## Common hawthorn *Crataegus monogyna*

This was number six in my collection and dates back to 1969. As I no longer own any of its predecessors, this tree has now been the longest in my possession. It therefore carries a lot of sentimental value.

I was first attracted by the natural curves in the trunk when I dug it out of a bank in a local brick factory. It must have been about five years old at the time and as far as I was concerned, it was a natural Bonsai needing no attention, so I planted it in a heavy blue and cream stoneware pot with a rock placed beside it. In time several adventitious buds formed and the tree sent out shoots in all directions. After two or three years I very much wanted a cascade style Bonsai so I decided to wire one of these branches into a downward curving line. This set the pattern for the tree and over the next few years secondary branches emanating from this major branch (now the trunk), were wired into aesthetically sympathetic positions. The design of the tree is full of movement and elegantly dynamic in mood and as long as the trunk remains thin, I shall continue refining the twigs and the foliage to perpetuate this image. So far this tree has flowered only once during the time I have owned it.

▲ 1971. This seedling hawthorn was collected in 1969 when it was barely six inches (15cm) high. It was originally the sixth tree in my collection and I was attracted by the natural twist in its trunk and thought at the time that it was a ready-made Bonsai.

▲ By 1979 the tree had been grown on for several years in a variety of pots and produced several long shoots. I decided to retain one, which I wire trained in a downward direction transforming the tree into a cascade style. It was re-potted into a tall earthenware pot especially made for it.

▲ Several new shoots grew in the following year which were in turn wired into position.

▲ In 1985 it was re-potted into a tall red stoneware pot, the tree is beginning to look more convincing with a better balanced foliage density. The crown is a bit heavy.

◀ On display at the National Bonsai Exhibition in 1986. The tree has been extensively thinned out and only leaves curving in the right direction have been retained. This sort of detailed refining is important when preparing trees for exhibition. The tree is displaying a good centre-of-gravity axis, which again is an important element to consider in the design of the Bonsai. The crown still needs further reduction to create an homogenous texture throughout the foliage.

## Hornbeam *Carpinus betulus*

This hornbeam was growing in some scree at the base of a steep rocky bank when I collected it. It has been trained as a root-over-rock semi-cascade Bonsai. To reinforce the dynamics of the semi-cascade style I have wired the trunk and branches so that they all reflect similar lines and direction: creating a sense of flow and movement.

These linear rhythms are better appreciated when the tree is in its winter state. Note too, how the trunk and branch lines reflect the round sweeping shape of the rock on which the tree is growing.

After the tree had been firmly tied to the rock, ample sphagnum moss was placed over the roots to protect them from drying out. Each year any branches that were growing in an opposite direction were pruned out. Hornbeams are notorious for their random growth patterns which produce branches in all manner of places and in every conceivable direction.

This tree is usually re-potted every three to four years. I have occasionally leaf-pruned it, but unless this action is executed early in the season the tree rarely produces a satisfactory second flush of leaves. Having found this to be the case with other hornbeams I now tend to leave the original leaves on for the whole of the summer. Leaf size can be better controlled by watering sparingly.

The leaves of hornbeams are prone to sun scorching, so are best situated in a semi-shaded area.

▼ *In 1986 the Bonsai was re-potted into a silver-fox grey 'yamaki' pot about which I am now having second thoughts. This tree undoubtedly looks better in its winter state. In summer the leaves conceal its rhythms and tend to create an over-heavy mass of foliage. Although hornbeams can be leaf pruned to reduce leaf size, they are not an ideal species for this technique. The diminishing taper in the trunk of this tree also supports its linear movement and visual flow.*

▼ A young collected hornbeam in 1973 with roots spread over a rock and covered in moss for protection from the sun's drying effect.

▲ By 1976 the trunk has been extended and trained into a semi-cascade style and the moss has been removed.

▲ 1980. Re-potted and further refined, the branches are each a reflection of the major trunk lines. Note too, how the trunk line reflects the curve in the rock so that the whole design interrelates.

# Larch *Larix decidua*

Unfortunately I do not have any early photographs of this Bonsai as it started its days as two matchstick-thin collected seedlings about five inches (12cm) tall. These seedlings were planted into a garden bed for three years to increase their size. They were then transplanted into a wooden fruit box and positioned carefully so that they related to each other. (Incidentally both trees would have made fine individual Bonsai but I had a very clear image in my mind of what I wanted to design.)

I removed most of the lower branches on both trunks and jinned them into short spurs. The branches were then wire-trained and the trees grown on to generate more secondary branches. These in turn were wired and positioned. The tree was then re-potted into a very shallow oval pot with the compost gently steeped up to give a little more soil for the roots. The primary and secondary trunks were deliberately placed side by side and this tended to have a flattening effect on the overall image which weakened the illusion of perspective. This was remedied at the next re-potting when the trees were rotated slightly in order that one trunk appeared slightly behind the other. As a result the foliage crowns then needed reorientating to create a new 'front'. It took two seasons to achieve this

In terms of living up to my mental image, I feel very satisfied with this Bonsai as it has responded to everything I have asked of it. One serious problem of the species is that the branches do tend in time to become excessively thick and knobbly with leaf buds. This makes it very difficult to control the sense of scale in the tree and the design will need to be re-evaluated every eight to ten years. However, this is a challenging and fascinating exercise which can add to your enjoyment when you create Bonsai with larch.

◄ 1978. *These two trees were collected several years earlier as matchstick thin seedlings about six inches (15cm) high. They were planted in a garden bed to gain size and although each would have made good single Bonsai, I had an image in my mind of twin larches which I wanted to create.*

► *After several years of training, the trees were re-potted in 1980 into a very shallow pot to compliment their height and enhance the concept of space.*

◄ *They were further refined in 1984 to improve the outline of the foliage canopy.*

► 1985. *Although the trees look reasonably balanced in their winter state, when they are in leaf the top becomes too dense.*

▶ In 1986 I thinned out the branches in the crown to reduce their visual weight and also introduced one or two more jins. The trees have been re-potted and slightly rotated to bring the major trunk in front of the secondary trunk. This is to improve the perspective and depth. It will need further reduction to the crown in future years and because of the new trunk positions, an undesirable bend in the primary trunk is visible. I have placed a clamp on it to correct this fault.

▲ The sketch shows how I may have to re-form the crown at a later date when the density of the foliage becomes grotesque. It is vital with literati style trees that elegance and lightness is maintained throughout the whole of the Bonsai.

## Workshop trees

This section illustrates the before and after stages of several trees that have been created by students attending my Bonsai workshops. They clearly demonstrate the need to take a radical approach to the structuring of Bonsai. You need to be able to find the line in the tree to create the final design and then have the courage to 'go through with the job'.

◄ Scots pine (var. Beuvronensis) purchased at a garden centre and brought along to one of my styling workshops by a student.

► The same tree has been pruned and wired into a triple trunk style which after four to five years will develop into a very handsome Bonsai.

◄ A student admiring a collected Scots pine which he has brought to the workshop.

► Three to four hours later, after very radical pruning, the tree has been trained into an upright style. Note the excellent taper in the trunk.

◄ This hefty Wellingtonia was dug up from one of my 'fattening up' garden beds and sold to a student. It had reached this size from a twelve-inch (30cm) cutting after only three growing seasons.

► This Potensai has been trained into a classical formal upright sequoia. Note how each branch has been wired down close to the trunk. The problem now is how do we get it back into the car to take it home?

▲ The seemingly 'impossible' sort of tree that is sometimes brought along to workshops by students.

▲ After discussing a number of possibilities, such as, 'It will soon be bonfire night' and, 'If you would like to leave now, I won't make any charge', we decided to remove all the branches from one side and wire all the others to form new 'trunks'. The tree was then turned over on its side, and the net result can be seen. (Incidentally the student who owned this tree is a very good friend of mine with a great sense of humour!)

◄ It was potted up and will eventually become a sweet little raft style hornbeam.

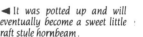

▲ A large imported Chinese juniper that was allowed to grow unchecked by its former owner. As a result it has become top heavy.

▲ We decided at the workshop to prune out several branches and restructure the tree in respect of the elegant trunk and bring height rather than breadth into its design. The crown of the tree and some of the rear branches towards the left-hand side still need to be wired to complete the job.

▲ This detail of one of the branches shows the emphasis that is placed on neat and well-executed wiring. We insist on this at workshop sessions.

# Associated techniques and culture

*Yellow, green, red, brown*
*the maple leaf's own rainbow*
*clouds alone are grey*

This chapter offers a number of additional techniques and practices associated with Bonsai and because of their miscellaneous nature they are not presented in any kind of order.

## Bonsai records and photo-notes

It will be obvious from the previous chapter that the careful documentation of any Bonsai, supported by the occasional photograph can prove most useful in the logging of its progress. Written notes not only supply a record of the tree but are a helpful reminder of the next stage in its development. (Refer to the Appendix on Annual Cycles on page 146.)

When photographing Bonsai, place the tree in front of a plain background wherever possible as this will make it easier to see the peripheral form of the tree. Avoid the use of

**Bonsai Record Card**

| COMMON NAME | BOTANICAL NAME | | AGE | DATE |
|---|---|---|---|---|
| STYLE | ORIGIN | | | |

FURTHER INFORMATION

▲ A *typical index card for filing Bonsai records*.

direct flash lights on your camera as this may cause distracting shadows around the tree. Always make a note of the date when the photograph was taken.

It would have been impossible for me to have written this book if I had not been meticulous in my photo-documentation of each tree. Photographs, unlike drawings, illustrate actuality and not just conjecture and are therefore usually more convincing in demonstrating a particular point. My sketches tend to express my romantic dreams for my trees!

## Tree faults

The illustrations show some of the classical faults to be avoided in the design of Bonsai — although many a Bonsai masterpiece is able to succeed visually in spite of having several of these faults. It is all entirely relative, and if aesthetic harmony can be achieved, it really does not matter too much how it happens. However, it is generally easier to organize a tree's structure into configurations of balanced space and form if you can use fault-free Potensai in the first place. This is a difficult debate to resolve and one that will remain controversial for as long as the art exists.

▲ *Root faults:* 1 'Knee' roots which rise up above soil level. 2 Excessively thick roots. 3 Aerial roots that do not ramify from around the root buttress. 4 Backward-growing and crossed roots. 5 Too many roots on one side of the trunk. 6 Chopped-off surface roots. 7 Tangled-up 'bird's-nest' roots.

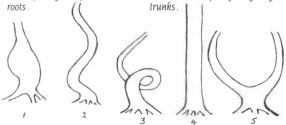

▼ *Trunk faults:* 1 Inverse taper with bulge. 2 Boring 'S' bends. 3 Spiralling trunks. 4 Parallel trunk with no taper. 5 'Frogs' leg' trunks.

► Branch faults: 1 Backward-growing branches. 2 Branches emanating from a concave bend in the trunk. 3 Spoke-wheel branches. 4 Bar branches. 5 Parallel branches. 6 Downward-growing comb branches. 7 Eye-poking branch. 8 Upward-growing comb branches. 9 Crossed branches. 10 Upward-curving 'C' branch. 11 'Y' branch. 12 Snake-bend branches. 13 Downward-curving 'C' branch. 14 Trunk-crossing branch.

# Under-plantings and the surface treatment of Bonsai

Bonsai composts can look rather stark unless dressed with some simple unobtrusive surface plants. Mosses in all their variety tend to be the most popular choice. Collect moss from walls, cracks in pavements, roofs etc and allow it to dry naturally. When the moss is dry, break it down to a powder (food liquidizers are ideal for this purpose), then sprinkle it over the surface of the compost in the Bonsai pot and water gently with a spray being careful not to wash the moss away. After a few weeks the moss will begin to grow. If it becomes too thick, then remove chunks of it from time to time. It is important to remember that if moss dries on the surface of pots it can

make watering rather difficult as the water tends to run off the surface of the moss. Should this happen, submerge the pot in a tub of water making sure it is thoroughly soaked.

Plants used for surface dressing should enhance the overall image and should never dominate the presentation. The use of under-plantings in Bonsai is very much a personal choice and not a routine practice. Many Bonsai purists refuse to countenance under-plantings. My own view is that they are best suited to the less formal styles and should be avoided if they are going to cause any serious distraction to the tree.

▲ Various mosses and dwarf saxifrages planted on a rock and soil surface.

▼ Moss under-planting.

▲ Dwarf rush (Acorus gramineus) planted at the base of the trunk on the side where there are no roots to offset the deficiency.

▼ Under-planting of Arenaria balearica.

▼ Under-planting of Raoulia australis on tufa rock.

# Accent plantings

Accent plantings, which should not be confused with under-plantings, are ancillary plantings of grasses, mosses, common weeds, small flowers, dwarf bamboos, rushes, sedges, alpines, cacti etc. They are used mostly in conjunction with Bonsai that are to be displayed formally. This can be in a *tokonoma* arrangement (described below) or often when Bonsai are shown in exhibitions.

Accent plantings are entirely informal in their arrangement and introduce all sorts of associated ideas. For instance they may be used to suggest a season, or perhaps create a natural mood. They may contrast a texture, or a colour, or a shape. It is important that they are allowed freedom of growth with minimum grooming. Accent plantings containing several different species in the same growing container can often be very effective. They also offer the opportunity to be a little more adventurous in the choice of the pot and the colour of the glaze.

▲ Variegated ornamental grass (Hachonechloa-macra aureola). It is customary to cut back grasses and bamboos each year to half an inch (13mm) in the early spring. This will encourage fresh new growth in the summer.

▲ Dwarf bamboo (Arundinaria pygmaea). Remove the dead leaves from time to time.

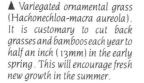

▲ Black mondo grass (Ophio-pogon planiscapus nigrescens).

◄ Blood grass (Imperata cylindrica). A beautiful variety of grass that starts its growth with green blades whose tips later turn a striking red.

◄ *The dandelion is a popular weed used in accent plantings.*

► *This cotoneaster 'hedge' is my little Bonsai joke which never fails to amuse. It is all too easy to become over serious in Bonsai so if possible one should maintain a sense of fun and humour otherwise the art becomes too intense and stressful. To satisfy my own perverse humour, I sometimes place a plastic reindeer or similar abomination beside the trunk of a Bonsai, just to raise the eyebrows of my friends. It's a wicked practice but I derive immense pleasure from studying their learned expressions. Forgive me, folks!*

▲ *Micro environments are also fun to create and can be used effectively as accent plantings. Here is one made from moss planted on tufa rock.*

▼ *Micro environment of cotoneasters, thyme and moss.*

▲ *Micro environment of cotoneasters and dwarf saxifrages.*

▲ Select an interesting piece of dead trunk or branch and make sure it is treated with a wood pre-server such as clear Cuprinol, then allow it to dry.

## Driftwood style 'wrap-arounds'

Driftwood style Bonsai can be simulated by using the trunk of an old dead tree which has an interesting line with plenty of jins on it. These dead trunks and even weathered branches can be found in the mountains and on beaches. The idea is to attach a living tree to it using the technique illustrated in this section. Because the tree that is to be attached is likely to be bent and twisted rather a lot, it is preferable to use young stock plants, and ideally, long whippy ones.

This technique works best with coniferous varieties but there are a number of deciduous species worth considering. The result tends to be rather abstract. The west-coast Americans use this technique extensively to produce Chinese juniper *Shimpaku* Bonsai on Californian juniper trunks. They sometimes use grafting techniques to do the same thing.

Here is a list of species that may be considered for the technique: needle juniper, common juniper, Chinese juniper, various pines, larch, yew, cedar, various cypresses, firethorn, hornbeam, jasmine, apricot and other

prunus species, Lonicera nitida (dwarf honeysuckle), birch, cotoneaster, oak, hawthorn, pomegranate, quince, rhododendrons and azaleas, willow, wisteria (just imagine the racemes of flowers — mind-blowing!), and possibly others. Some of these species may seem a little far-fetched but this is a good way of achieving some very interesting abstract sculptural tree forms, and often one tree species can be used to suggest another. For instance juniper species can be used to create pine-like Bonsai. This may not necessarily be the purest of approaches to Bonsai but it certainly offers plenty of scope for imagination and innovation.

With a little patience the technique can be very successful and well worth trying but do make sure the piece of driftwood that is selected in the first place has plenty of interest and character or a lot of time may be wasted and the net result may be somewhat boring.

The best time to attempt this technique is in spring when the Potensai shows signs of awakening from winter dormancy.

▲, Some of the materials required to make up the base: car-body filler paste with hardener, wire, chicken mesh, wire cutter, old knife, jinning tool or pliers, poly-thene sheet and toilet paper or rag.

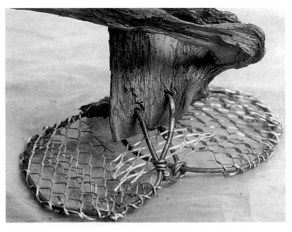

▶ Drill some holes through the base of the wood and attach wire and chicken mesh to form a 'foot' to enable the trunk to stand up easily.

▲ Mix sufficient car-body filler with a little of the hardening agent according to the manu-facturer's instructions.

▶ Spread the filler over the chicken mesh and slightly up the base of the trunk with the knife making sure it is worked well into the fissures of the wood.

▼ When dry, drill several holes through the base with a high speed drill not less than one quarter of an inch (7 mm) in diameter. This is for the roots to grow through and to help with the drainage.

▲ Treat the whole of the trunk with a solution of lime sulphur or domestic bleach to preserve and bleach the wood and allow it to dry. This action and the previous stage should all have been executed well in advance of the next stage — that is, the attaching of the Potensai to the piece of wood. In fact it is a good idea to prepare pieces of driftwood in this way in the winter months when there is little else to do.

◀ Select a 'whippy' Potensai to attach to the driftwood. In this case the tree is a needle juniper which was made from a cutting and which has spent a couple of seasons growing in a garden bed.

▲ With a very sharp grafting knife cut a slither of bark and some of the underlying sapwood along one side of the Potensai. The removal of the bark in this way causes the future developing callous to spread itself better as the tree attaches itself to the driftwood, making the final result more convincing:

▲ The bark has been removed along the whole of one side of the Potensai.

► Protect the Potensai with bits of sponge sheet before strapping it tightly to the piece of wood. Make sure it is positioned where it will appear to advantage when the tree is finally trained into a Bonsai.

◄ An alternative tying technique is to use electrical cable straps which are much easier to use bu add to the overall cost.

► Apply a coating of grafting wax along both sides of the attached tree to reduce any tendency for the cut areas to dry out. This wax coating also protects the cut areas from insect and fungal attack. Trim back the tie 'tails'.

▲ Spray the roots with water frequently throughout the whole performance to prevent them from drying out or the whole exercise will be wasted. Alternatively wrap the roots up in a damp rag.

► The tree attached along its entire length.

▲ Give the roots a soaking in a mild vitamin B1-enriched solution of water using Superthrive or an equivalent compound to encourage the initiation of roots when the Potensai is potted up.

▼ It is most important that a good drainage course of grit or chippings is placed over the bottom of the pot and that a well-draining compost is used when planting the tree.

▲ The potted-up driftwood style Potensai 'wrap-around'. Protect it from the wind and from strong sunlight and, if possible, place it in a humid environment for the first few weeks of training.

◄ Here is the same tree two growing seasons later. Note that growth has been encouraged by regular fertilizing to thicken the attached trunk. The Potensai offers a number of possibilities for the final arrangement of the branches. It will be allowed to grow on unchecked for a further year or two during which time I shall continue fertilizing and watering well.

▼ These sketches show a variety of ways in which the branches and foliage can be trained to achieve different tree forms with their respective dynamics.

## Glass-fibre fabrications

To illustrate how glass-fibre can be used very successfully in a number of Bonsai applications I have taken as my example a customized pot for a collected common juniper. Although the end product of this sequence is a simulated stone crescent pot the technique can be adapted to all manner of variations — for example to create artificial rocks, landscapes, slabs, pools, driftwood or *suiseki*.

Make sure when working with glass-fibre and epoxy resins that there is plenty of ventilation, as strong-smelling fumes are generated by the process.

Furthermore, avoid working on cold, damp days as this will impede the drying out of the resin.

All sorts of additives can be mixed into the resin to bulk it up and make the process more economic but make sure that anything that is added is perfectly dry. When painting the finished product it is best to use matt cellulose-based paints as they become integrated with the resin body. Emulsion and oil–based paints are likely to flake off in time.

One of the main advantages of the process is that containers or slabs can be produced for specific trees and therefore their dimensions and shapes can be carefully controlled.

▲ A collected common juniper which has undergone some basic training and is now in need of a new pot. I have decided to make a crescent pot for the tree to suggest a symbolic cliff face out of which the tree is to grow. The upper reaches of the tree will be jinned as my 'supporting story' suggests they will be exposed to the ravages of cliff-top winds. This storyline will be the concept for my design.

▲ Bend a piece of wire to suggest the outline of the crescent pot and place it up against the tree to confirm its shape.

► Cut out some chicken-mesh to the approximate size of the pot and bend it into shape.

▼ Wrap some rags around the wire to simulate foliage.

▼ Place the simulated wire tree in the mesh pot and try it for size. Make any necessary adjustments to its shape at this stage.

◄ Cut out some convenient sized pieces of glass fibre matting and place them on the inside of the mesh. Then with a nylon bristle brush apply some epoxy resin with an appropriate amount of hardening agent. Refer to the manufacturer's instructions for the correct proportion.

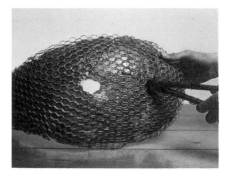

► When the whole of the inside of the mesh has been lined and dried out, cut out two drainage holes with wire cutters.

► Place a couple of stoppers in the holes to protect them. (In this case I have used two plastic 35mm film canisters.) Then mix up some cement filler (such as Polyfilla for exterior use) with coarse grit and water.

▲ Place the pot over any suitable support and spread a half-inch (13mm) covering of the cement mix over it. This is to act as a spacer and to give the pot some weight.

▲ When the cement has dried remove the drainage hole stoppers and make up some legs with more of the cement mix to provide a stable support for the pot and also to provide adequate ventilation under the pot.

▼ When the feet have dried, turn the pot over and stand it up. If necessary make further adjustments to the feet to achieve the correct standing position.

▲ Now paint the inside of the pot with epoxy resin.

▲ Apply some more glass-fibre matting to complete the 'sandwich' and use the end of the brush to stipple it in firmly. When this has dried, cut or file away any whiskers of glass fibre. Do make sure that the cement filler has been completely covered all round.

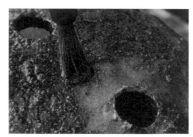

▲ Mix up some coarse grit with a solution of epoxy resin, paint over the whole of the pot to create a textured surface and allow it to dry.

◄ The finished pot with some cans of matt cellulose paint that I have selected to create a rusty brown iron colour.

◄ The finished painted pot. The whole process can take several days or even weeks to complete. It will depend a lot on the time it takes for the resin to dry. Do not be tempted to add more than the recommended amount of hardener to the resin as this will cause it to overheat and become brittle. The above technique can be adapted for all sorts of applications associated with Bonsai.

◄ I planted the juniper into the crescent pot in the following spring having first refined it by additional pruning and wiring. Note that I have also included several under-plantings to enhance the 'natural' effect. Looking at this photograph, I now feel the tree would have looked better if it had been planted a little further to the left.

In Japan the 'tokonoma' is an alcove in the home used for the formal display of certain artefacts or plants that warrant appreciation. It is the perfect platform for displaying Bonsai. The *tokonoma* invariably contains the combination of a hanging scroll, a Bonsai and an accent planting. Occasionally the accent planting is substituted for a *suiseki* (viewing stone) or a little figure — which may be human or animal. Whatever artefacts are used to support the Bonsai in its display, simplicity and formality are the essence of the exercise. Understatement is very important. The scroll should be muted in

## The *Tokonoma*

▲ *A typical 'tokonoma' arrangement of scroll, Bonsai and accent planting.*

colour and content and, to obey the strict rules of the *tokonoma*, should be placed exactly in the middle of the alcove. The Bonsai should be to one side of

the scroll and the accent planting on the other side where it completes the overall balance within an asymmetric triangle. Like *ikebana* flower arrangements, the three elements displayed in the *tokonoma* represent heaven, earth and man. The scroll represents heaven, the accent planting represents earth and the Bonsai is the reconciling element, man.

It is difficult to construct an authentic *tokonoma* in the average western home as it requires all sorts of architectural disciplines. So you invariably have to compromise and make do with a suitable plain wall fronted with a low dais on which to place the Bonsai and accent planting.

## Suiseki

▲ *Mountain stone: a form of marble found by a friend of mine in Scotland.*

◀ *Island stones made up from pieces of wind-eroded sandstone found in Pembrokeshire, Wales.*

▲ *Serpentine mountain stone found in Cornwall.*

▶ *Tall sandstone mountain on carved mahogany stand. I have finished the carving and polished the stand since this photograph was taken.*

▲ *Waterfall stone set amongst tufa overgrown with moss and incorporating a sand lake.*

▶ *Sandstone rock suggesting a range of snow-clad mountains, given to me by a friend.*

*Suisekis* are probably best described as 'viewing stones'. That is, stones that suggest specific views such as mountains, islands, waterfalls, lakes, plateaux, house stones etc. It will of course depend on the impression suggested by the individual stone. On the other hand it may just be a beautiful piece of rock worthy of appreciation.

Good *suiseki* are very much prized by their owners and can be of high value. They can be displayed in shallow pans known as *suibans* or occasionally on wooden stands carved to suit the individual stone. Searching for *suiseki* during a holiday can be great fun often leading to moments of ecstacy when a fine example is found!

*Suisekis* are often used instead of an accent planting in *tokonoma* displays, and it is a sobering thought to know that most *suiseki* existed on this planet long before man.

# Bonsai calendar

*Wet wet day all wet*
*summer is crying aloud*
Bonsai needs no hose

This chapter offers a month-by-month breakdown of tasks associated with Bonsai. In order that it can be adapted for the southern hemisphere as well as the northern hemisphere I have qualified the months with their appropriate seasons. The routines suggested may be further modified to suit local conditions and indigenous tree species.

## January or mid-winter

A bleak time in the year when the garden is usually most uninviting. It will require a good deal of self discipline to carry out all of the necessary chores. Your trees should have been stowed away in their winter quarters by now to protect them against frost and severe winds. Remember that winds can cause the soil in the pots to dry out very quickly so do make sure your trees are watered as necessary and never allowed to dry out completely. It is preferable to water in the morning as freshly watered pots can easily freeze if they have been watered in the evening.

This is a good month to update your Bonsai records and to plan the training regimes for the rest of the year. Study your deciduous trees closely whilst they are leafless and plan any necessary pruning to improve their form. Towards the end of the month you can apply a second insecticide spraying of a proprietary tar oil to asphyxiate any hibernating bugs and any insect eggs. Follow the manufacturer's instructions to obtain the correct dilution rate and protect the compost from the spray by placing some polythene over it.

If there is a mild spell during the month, you can dig over a garden bed and at the same time mix in some manure or leaf mould to expose it to the action of frost which will help to break down the heavy lumps in the soil and generally produce a more friable texture. This bed can be used for planting any Potensai you may collect from the wild in later months, or it may be useful as a 'fattening up' bed for cuttings etc.

During the long dark evenings it would make sense to prepare the artificial bases with car-body filler on pieces of driftwood if you intend creating any Bonsai 'wrap-arounds', and also to bleach them with a solution of lime sulphur. You may further occupy the time by carving wooden bases for some of your *suiseki* viewing stones.

January need not be an entirely glum month; you can invite your Bonsai friends around for a meal or two and spend many a happy hour enthusing about your Bonsai dreams for the coming spring and summer. A great deal can be learned from discussion with others and from shared ideas. It is also a great excuse to imbibe a dram or two of malt whisky or even down a jar of real ale. These shared moments with friends provide the warmth and reminiscences of times immemorial; of halcyon moments.

Conifers can be given a small quantity of weak fertilizer this month, and grafting should be undertaken towards the end of January.

## February or late winter

In early February if the soil is not too hard from the cold, sprinkle a soil pesticide over the surface of the compost to kill off any leatherjackets and other soil pests that may have hatched from eggs laid in the late summer.

This is also a good month to prepare for the imminent potting season. Make training pots out of reclaimed timber from old drawers, fruit boxes, floorboards etc and treat them with a wood preservative such as horticultural Cuprinol or equivalent. Make sure adequate drainage is provided and that there is a space under the container to permit ample ventilation. Check your ceramic pots for their suitability for specific trees and after cleaning them, place plastic drainage mesh over the drainage holes and wire it into position. This will save precious time when potting up your trees in the spring.

Potting composts should be mixed this month and stowed in open containers. I use large plastic wine casks with their tops sawn off as they are ideal for this purpose.

Early sprouting species such as the Japanese mountain maple variety, *kyo hime*, can be re-potted towards the end of February, but be sure to protect it from wind and frost.

## March or early spring

This is a good time in the year to collect Potensai from the wild but do obtain permission from the landowner before digging up any trees.

Update your Bonsai records and take photographs of trees that are scheduled for any structural changes. straighten out any reclaimed training wire so that it can be used again and sharpen all your Bonsai tools. Rake over prepared garden beds removing any stones and debris so that they will be ready for collected material.

Potting up Potensai and re-potting established Bonsai can begin as soon as there are signs of swelling in the buds. If mountain maples are to be pruned radically it is as well to root prune at the same time to reduce their tendency to 'bleed' after branch pruning.

Display benches should be scrubbed down and when dry they can be given a routine painting with a wood preservative such as creosote.

Single out any Bonsai you consider may be suitable for exhibiting later in the year and make sure they are placed in a particularly well protected part of the garden so that as their new leaves emerge next month they will not be damaged by any of the elements.

◀ *Mosses under snow.*

## April or mid-spring

Complete any re-potting. Check all trees for pests, particularly greenfly, and treat as necessary. Also check for any winter damage. Prepare under-plantings for trees scheduled for exhibition.

As the air temperature warms, gradually introduce your trees to the display benches but keep a watch out for frost and protect as necessary.

Apply second fertilizer to conifers and first fertilizer to any trees that have not been freshly potted. It is still too soon for them.

Seeds can be planted this month and conifer air-layerings can be initiated. Any air-layerings that were initiated last year that have developed sufficient roots by now can be severed from the parent plant and potted up into training pots. Tidy up accent plantings and re-pot it necessary. Trim back grasses and bamboos to encourage new growth.

All conifers can be given a routine preventative spraying of insecticide followed by a spraying of fungicide a fortnight later.

Be sure to add a drop or two of washing-up liquid to the sprays to improve penetration. Deciduous trees can be similarly sprayed but make sure this is done before any leaves have opened or the sprays are likely to cause the leaves to curl up and have an arthritic appearance.

Bonsai 'wrap-around' can be initiated this month. Also remove any wire that has been used for training trunks and branches and so on if it has done its job successfully.

Attend any Bonsai workshops available in your area.

▼ *Spruce needles.*

## May or late spring

A very active and exciting month for Bonsai enthusiasts. Trees can be safely displayed on the benches. Trees scheduled for exhibition should be protected against strong sunlight and leaf-scorching winds. Routine fertilizing programmes related to the species and age of the tree should now be underway and spraying against pests and diseases should also be undertaken. If appropriate, the leaf pruning of deciduous trees can be done in late May.

Routine grooming of trees and light wiring of new growth can be commenced.

Water young developing trees abundantly but give only enough water to sustain life and vigour to older trees. This will ensure their leaves do not grow too large.

Check the progress of any seeds that may have been sown in April and harden off developing seedlings. Give ample manure to developing trees in garden beds and keep a check on the weeds.

Scrub green algae off the trunks and branches of your Bonsai with an old toothbrush and clean water.

## June or early summer

Leaf prune and wire train all deciduous trees as necessary and continue the fertilizing regimes. Be especially watchful for insect attacks and spray accordingly. This is a good time to initiate air-layerings of deciduous species and to take softwood cuttings from freshly ripened growth.

Finger-pinch coniferous shoots to maintain the form of the tree if appropriate. Check under-plantings and prune back if too vigorous. Keep exhibition trees in semi-shade to prevent leaf scorching and to improve leaf colour.

Display your trees and accent plantings to their best advantage on the staging benches and relax with a cool beer or bowl of strawberries and cream as you absorb the sun and the compliments of all of your friends. This is a time to wallow and glory in your 'horti-aesthetic' achievements. A time to reflect on whether you have achieved your goals and also to project your thinking to future plans. A time to lie back on the lawn and listen to the summer. A happy time!

## July or mid-summer

Update your Bonsai records and take photographs of any significant changes that might have affected the trees. Pay close attention to the watering of your trees this month as they can easily dry out. This is particularly important if you have used the Mark two compost which is very free draining and has no humus content. At this time of the year the trees will benefit from frequent sprayings with water but do not do this when the sun is shining on the foliage as scorching of the leaves will result. Early evening is the best time to spray the trees.

Prune back any excessively long shoots to respect the overall shape of the trees and pay meticulous attention to the grooming and preparation of any trees to be exhibited. Most Bonsai exhibitions in England tend to take place between June and late August. Make sure the Bonsai pots are scrubbed clean before exhibiting the trees.

Sprinkle a soil pesticide over the compost to kill off any remaining leatherjackets that may have escaped the last treatment. Watch out for other pests and diseases and treat if necessary.

Check all seedlings and re-pot them into individual pots once they have produced their first pair of true leaves.

Willows, alders and other moisture-loving trees may be placed in basins of water to keep their roots cool and to provide better humidity for their foliage. Remove any dead flowers from azaleas and rhododendrons so as to prevent the seed pods from developing as these will take a lot of the vigour out of the tree if allowed to grow.

Make sure all weeds are removed as they appear in the pots and keep a check on the weeds in the growing-on garden beds.

If you go away on holiday, make sure that arrangements have been made with a responsible person to look after your trees. When on holiday, look out for *suiseki* and pieces of driftwood that can be used for 'wrap-arounds'.

This is an excellent time to construct glass-fibre pots and other containers as the warm air will dry out the epoxy resin fairly rapidly. It is also a good time to create jins and sharis on driftwood style Bonsai.

▼ *Flowers of the blackthorn (Prunus spinosa).*

## August or late summer

Now is the time to ease up on the fertilizing programmes and change over to fertilizers with less nitrogen and more phosphorus. This will help ripen any fruit and strengthen the root systems of your trees.

Depending on specific requirements, pines will have had their candles pruned throughout the summer. Refer to the section on pine pruning on page 70 to determine the particular technique ·that should be used. This is a good time for major pruning and wire training of pines and other coniferous species. If very radical pruning is undertaken on any of the genetic dwarf pine varieties, do make sure they are provided with winter protection later.

## September or early autumn

Fertilizing and watering can be cut right down to a minimum.

At this time of the year there is a tendency for the trunks and the branches of many species of tree, particularly the pines, to swell up quite dramatically, so do look out for wires that might be biting into the bark and remove them if this is the case. Continue the general pruning and shaping of your trees to maintain the best outlines and foliage contours.

Check any air-layerings that might have been started earlier in the year and if they have produced sufficient roots sever them from their parent plants and pot up. Treat as giant cuttings and provide winter protection by way of a cold greenhouse. If there is still insufficient root production, it would be better to leave them until the following spring. Also check any cuttings you may have made and if roots have formed, transplant them into individual pots. These too should have winter protection.

It may make sense to enrol for an evening class in pottery or woodwork for the winter at your local institute for education. This could provide a means of making pots or display stands for your Bonsai. Check the condition of your Bonsai display benches and undertake any necessary repairs.

Once again, join any Bonsai workshops that may be available in your locality.

▶ *Maple leaves in autumn.*

### October or mid-autumn

Stop all nitrogenous fertilizing and apply a single phosphorus enriched fertilizer in mid-October.

This is a good time to collect seeds from the wild. Maples in particular are a good source and they should be planted straight away in seed pans and left outside for the whole of the winter. Make sure they are protected from hungry mice.

Check your pot requirements for next year and begin looking out for suitable ones to buy. It is not too early to start dropping hints to the family that Christmas is only a couple of months off. Incidentally Bonsai books also make good presents — particularly this one!

Check all wires that have been used in training and remove any that have done their job or that are biting into the bark.

Now is the time to buy in the various ingredients for next year's composts and to make sure any special materials, such as polythene sheeting etc, are purchased for use as winter protection.

The leaves on your deciduous trees will start to fall off as will some of the pine needles. Remove them from the pot surfaces to maintain a tidy state.

Check developments in the garden beds and decide which trees can be transplanted next year to commence their training for Bonsai and start thinking about possible styles they would suit.

Place your orders for any tree seeds you may like to sow next spring.

### November or late autumn

Update your Bonsai records. All trees can be given a final fertilizing for the year with some bonemeal. This is a slow-acting feed that will begin to release its nutrients in the following spring.

Although the atmosphere is likely to be very damp at this time of the year it will still be necessary to check that the soil in the pots has not dried out. Water as necessary to keep the trees just perceptibly damp. Avoid wet or soggy conditions. Most trees will be well into a state of dormancy by now.

Any hard-shelled seeds that you have purchased can be stratified (see page 82) to improve germination when they are sown next spring. Tidy up the display benches and the garden generally but leave fallen leaves on the garden beds. They will help protect the roots of any of the planted out trees from frost and, as the leaves decompose, they will also provide humus and nutrients for the soil.

Towards the end of this period spray all the deciduous trees with a proprietary tar-oil compound to asphyxiate any hibernating bugs etc that might be lurking in amongst the branches of the trees. Be sure to protect the compost from this spray as it leaves an unsightly oily deposit.

Tidy up the Bonsai workshop and make sure all tools are cleaned and oiled before they are stowed away for the winter. Check up on your stocks of fertilizers, insecticides, fungicides, plant labels, composts etc and list any deficiencies. Add these to your Christmas present hints, and if Father Christmas proves to be a little unsympathetic then replace the deficiencies early in the new year yourself!

### December or early winter

This is one of the quietest and least active of months in the Bonsai calendar. Routine checks should be made on all your trees from time to time to confirm that all is well with them. Make sure that evergreen species such as firethorns and holm oaks etc (as well as coniferous species) are situated so that they still receive plenty of light or the chlorophyll level will drop in their leaves making them much more vulnerable to infection from pests and diseases.

This is a good time to catch up on your Bonsai reading. You can study pictures of some of the Bonsai masterpieces and hopefully apply some of the styles to your own trees, or you can single out certain trees that you particularly admire and plan a reconstruction exercise for next year with some of your own Potensai. You can learn a great deal about Bonsai structure and technique by doing this.

If you are a member of a Bonsai society you could spare a thought for its society journal or newsletter and perhaps write an article or two for it. If you are not a member of a society, then it would undoubtedly be to your advantage to join one. Most Bonsai societies can be located through your local information centre, or in Great Britain, through the Federation of British Bonsai Societies.

## Conclusion

The saying 'The more one learns, the more one knows there is to learn' is certainly true of Bonsai. I know that as my trees progress each year so does my experience, and as a result I appreciate that improvements can always be made to them. I therefore strive to keep an open mind with regard to their styles and form. If any changes need to be made, I weigh up the 'pros and cons' of each before effecting any necessary improvements. This continual reappraisal of the state of the art is what is so challenging and exciting about it. It is as I suggested earlier, an art with a fourth dimension — the dimension of life. The life of the tree is entwined with the life of the Bonsai enthusiast who has the capacity to adapt and re-adapt to the changes of time and space; of philosophy and experience.

Whether I have wanted it or not, Bonsai has always been for me, a way of life. Through it I have found a means in which I can express any notions I may have on form and space. In pursuit of this I have realised that Bonsai, at its best, is the distillation and application of aesthetics and horticulture practised with excellence and dedication and committed to the production of the harmony between truth and beauty.

I began this book with a poem, so perhaps it would be fitting to end with one.

Yesterday they came, and there is life;
Tomorrow they will go, and there is death;
But today they perceive;
and there is experience.

Bonsai is for today; enjoy the experience,
or better still, experience the joy!

# Appendix one
# Annual cycles
## based on a five-year planner

Early misty morn
damp leaves smoulder through the day
autumn filled nostrils

In this appendix I have provided a number of examples of how the Bonsai Planner can be used. I have taken as examples a typical coniferous species and a typical deciduous species to illustrate the planner in use. One 'circuit' grid has been deliberately left blank. You can duplicate this grid as many times as you like and use it in conjunction with your own trees.

You will notice too that I have left a few blank spaces in the reference key. This is so that you can incorporate any additional instructions that I may have omitted to suit your own personal requirements.

By planning a programme in this way you not only create a diary of tasks needing attention but also end up with an accurate record of the tree and its treatment.

Obviously the Planner has its limitations and it can be used only in certain applications. For instance it indicates only *when* to do certain things and not *how* to do them. It will therefore be necessary to use it in conjunction with the Bonsai Calendar and the various techniques described in the book. This is particularly the case when indicating the most suitable fertilizers to use and, in these examples, the bracketed letters following the symbol indicate the recommended fertilizer in order of preference or for use in a rotational programme. (See the section on fertilizers on page 36.)

I have included in the reference key an aphabetic as well as a symbolic reference so that you can use either when planning your own Bonsai requirements. The task associated with the respective symbol is

graphically much easier to recognize and remember than a letter of the alphabet. On the other hand, you may have difficulty in drawing the symbols and prefer to use the alpha reference.

Of course there is nothing to stop you recording whatever information you like in the grid, provided it serves your purpose.

Although the months of the year have been indicated for users in the northern hemisphere, the grid can be adapted by using the background colour coding instead. That is: blue for winter; yellow for spring; green for summer and orange for autumn. By relating these colour/seasons to the corresponding months in your own country you can adapt it accordingly.

This may seem very complicated at first, but with a little patience you will soon get into the swing of things and appreciate that the grid can give you the opportunity to cram a vast amount of information into a relatively small space.

## Key

| Symbol | Letter | Description |
|---|---|---|
| | A | Pot up |
| | B | Re-pot/root-prune |
| | C | Re-pot/root prune every five years |
| | D | Feed fortnightly — for vigorous growth |
| | E | Feed monthly — to stabilize growth and vigour |
| | F | Feed bi-monthly — to minimize growth but maintain health |
| | G | Water abundantly — to encourage maximum growth and vigour |
| | H | Water sparingly — to minimize growth but maintain health |
| | I | Prune — for structure — main branches and/or trunk |
| | J | Prune — for refinement — twigs and foliage |
| | K | Wire train — to establish main structure of trunk and primary branches |
| | L | Wire train — for twig and foliage detail |
| | M | Remove wires that have done their job |
| | N | Protect from wind and frost |
| | O | Pests and diseases — check for and treat as necessary |
| | P | Update records and/or photograph trees |
| | Q | Grow on in garden bed to increase size |
| | R | Transplant from garden bed to training pot |
| | S | Other instruction: |
| | T | Other instruction: |

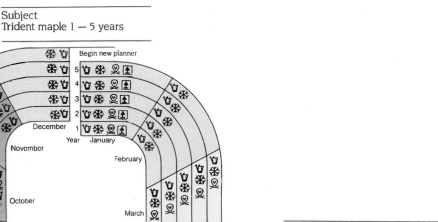

Subject
**Trident maple 1 — 5 years**

Begin new planner

Subject
**Trident maple 6 years — 10 years**

Subject
**Trident maple 11 years — 15 years**

Return to year 5 and continue cycles

NB   Make sure pots drain well
     Never let pots dry out

Bonsai planner

Subject

Date

Copyright waiver on this page: Please photostat
this planner and use it for your own programmes

NB   Make sure pots drain well
     Never let pots dry out

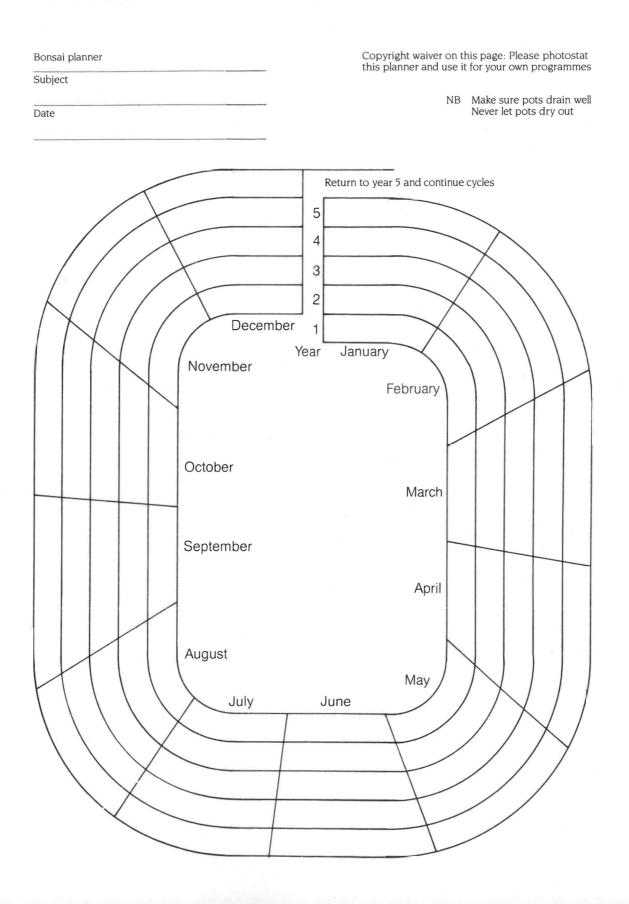

Return to year 5 and continue cycles

5
4
3
2
1

December

Year    January

November

February

October

March

September

April

August

May

July        June

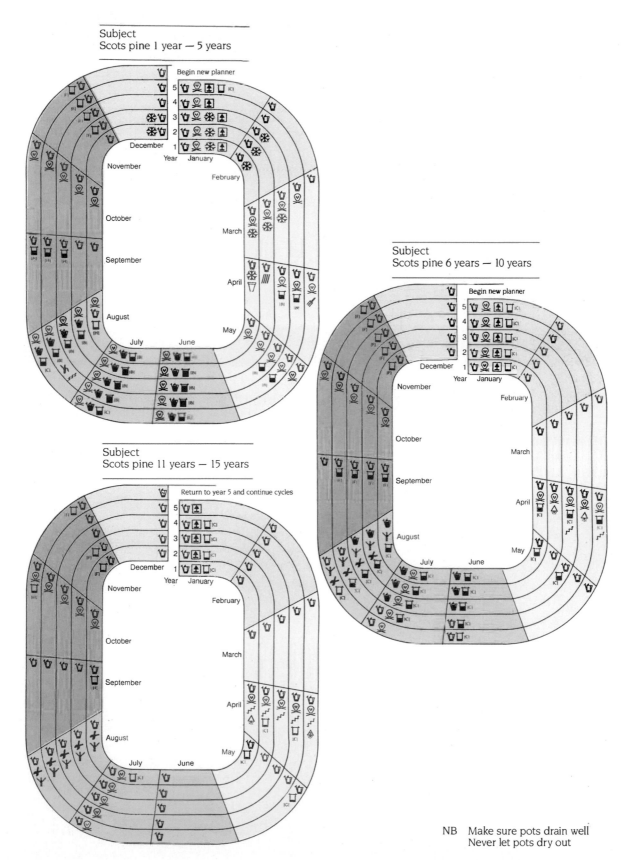

Subject
Scots pine 1 year — 5 years

Subject
Scots pine 6 years — 10 years

Subject
Scots pine 11 years — 15 years

NB   Make sure pots drain well
     Never let pots dry out

# Appendix two
# Suitable species for Bonsai

Who sees the tears
of the lonely golden carp
golden carp alone

In this appendix I have listed a selection of the most popular species of trees and shrubs used in the creation of Bonsai. There are of course many other trees that may be used but the ones listed here are the trees most generally available in the UK.

Wherever possible I have chosen to use the common name of the species unless I have wished to be absolutely specific; then I have included the Latin name as well. Occasionally, the Latin name is the common name. For example, azalea, rhododendron, cryptomeria etc. Because of this, I have tended to classify in alphabetical order the name most commonly used. To save confusion I have included in brackets the species for your further reference. For example: **Ivy** (Hedera spp), Hedera refers to the species to which Ivy belongs.

There are several species that have many sub-species or cultivars and in some instances I have been general in discussing them, whereas in other cases I have included some of the varieties. Do please refer to other books which supply standard references on trees and shrubs where I have included only a name with no description, and use these references in conjunction with this appendix.

## Star rating and categories

Although some people would argue that a Bonsai can be created from any species of tree, most would agree that certain species are more suitable than others. I have therefore indicated an order of preference based on my own experiences by using a star rating as follows:

\*\*\*\*\*
Classical species; ideally suitable for Bonsai

\*\*\*\*
Very good, but not a classic

\*\*\*
Good, but may provide some problems

\*\*
Fairly good; favoured by some people

\*
Dubious; may be worth trying, but not for me

There are three further categories rated thus:

M
Ideally suitable for 'mame' (bean sized) and 'shohin' (small) Bonsai

B
Ideal for beginners

!
Grown for its curiosity or novelty value

Wherever possible, I have supplied information about the trees in the following manner:

## Key

**Common name (a)** of tree or shrub/star rating/other category

**Description (b)** of tree or shrub; may also include varieties or cultivars

**Source (c)** from whence Potensai can be obtained in order of priority

**Styles (d)** most suitable for this species

**Compost (e)** most suitable for this species

**Situation (f)** related to weather

**Pot (g)** most suitable for this species

## Selection of species

*Acer/ maple (Acer spp) A large family of very suitable species for developing into Bonsai.*

a **Trident maple** (Acer buergerianum) \*\*\*\*\*/M/B
b *Deciduous tree of medium size with three-lobed leaves that colour up beautifully in autumn. Refined twigs; good roots; interesting bark.*
c *Imports; air-layers; cuttings; seeds.*
d *All, and particularly root-over-rock. Avoid coiled style, twisted trunk and exposed root.*
e *Mk1 or Mk2*
f *Protect from wind and excessive sunlight in summer. Protection from frost and ice essential in winter.*
g *Most shapes with glazes that compliment the autumn foliage colours.*

a *Japanese mountain maple (Acer palmatum)* \*\*\*\*\*/M/B
b *Medium-sized hardy deciduous tree with five-lobed sharply pointed leaves. Many sub-species. NB: several of the pink and red sub-species are half-hardy, eg. 'seigen', 'deshojo', 'shin-deshojo', 'chishio', 'chishio' improved. All display spectacular autumn colour. The variety 'kyo hime' is one of the first trees to break winter dormancy.*
c *Imports; container-grown; air-layers; graftings; cuttings; seed.*
d *All*
e *Mk1 or Mk2.*
f *The pink and red varieties need winter protection. All varieties should be protected from wind and excessive sunlight.*
g *Mostly glazed ovals and soft-edged rectangular shapes.*

a *Field maple (Acer campestre)* \*\*/M/B
b *Deciduous tree of medium size. Five-lobed rounded leaves. Stiff twigs.*
c *Collected wildlings; air-layers; container-grown.*
d *All, best suited to larger Bonsai.*
e *Lime tolerant. Mk1.*
f *Hardy, but provide some protection from sun.*
g *Glazed oval, rectangular.*

a **Alder** (Alnus spp) **/M/B
b Medium-sized tree often found
growing beside rivers. Large
dark black-green obovate leaves
with prominent ribs and very
dark brown-black bark.
c Collected wildlings.
d Informal upright; broom;
slanting.
e Mk1 with added peat kept
very damp.
f Semi-shade in summer.
g Shallow glazed round or oval.

a **Apricot** (Prunus spp)
*****/M
b Medium-sized tree with pink
or white flowers that open in
early spring; occasionally it
fruits. Very attractive.
c Imports; container-grown;
grafting.
d Most, but especially
split-trunk; literati; broom;
informal upright; slanting.
e Mk1.
f Full sun. Provide winter
protection.
g Ornamental glazed
rectangular or oval; slabs;
crescents.

a **Arbutus or strawberry tree**
(Arbutus spp) **/!
b Medium-sized evergreen
broadleaf tree that produces a
curious fruit somewhat like a
strawberry.
c Container-grown;
air-layering.
d Informal upright; slanting;
hollow trunk.
e Mk1
f Provide winter protection.
g Oval; rectangular; circular,

a **Ash** (Fraxinus spp) **/B
b Large deciduous tree with
pinnate leaves and thick stiff
twigs.
c Collected wildlings.
d Informal upright; slanting;
groups; split or hollow trunk;
clump.
e Mk1.
f Entirely hardy.
g Rectangular; square; oval.

a **Bamboo** (see below spp)
*****/!
b Grass-like plant mostly with
hollow stems and lanceolate
leaves. Very varied in colour and
size (from one or two inches
(5cm) to scores of feet).
Available species are:
Arundinaria; Chusquea;
Phyllostachys; Sasa; Shibatea.
Each has several sub-species
but the Sasas and

Arundinarias are the most
popular.
c Division of culms;
container-grown; imports.
d Accent plantings.
e Mk1 plus additional loam and
leaf mould kept very damp.
f Protect from wind, sun and
frost.
g Shallow pots or slabs.

a **Beech** (Fagus sylvatica;
Fagus crenata) *****/M/B
b Large deciduous tree with
smooth bark and thin green
leathery leaves. Also
copper-coloured varieties.
c Collected wildlings;
container-grown; air-layering.
d Upright; informal upright;
forest groups; windswept;
clump; twin-trunk; split-trunk;
broom; raft.
e Lime tolerant. Mk1.
f Leaves scorch easily in strong
sunlight. Provide semi-shade.
g Rectangular; oval; circular;
slabs.

a **Berberis** (especially
B. Darwinii) ****/B/!
b Evergreen shrub with shiny
dark green prickly leaves not
unlike miniature holly leaves.
Pretty flowers and clusters of
deep purple berries.
c Large unwanted garden
specimens pruned back hard to
about eighteen inches (46cm);
large air-layerings from garden
specimens.
d Very suitable for split or
hollow-trunk styles. Use
chainsaw to assist carving.
e Mk1.
f Provide winter protection.
g Oval; circular.

a **Silver birch** (Betula spp)
****/M/B
b Graceful tree with
silvery-white bark, delicate
branches and small leaves.
Many sub-species including:
Jacquemontii; Papyrifera and
the dwarf variety: Nana.
c Collected wildlings;
container-grown; air-layerings;
graftings; seed; cuttings.
d All except stump style. Very
good for growing over rock as
they have a robust root system.
e Mk1 or Mk2.
f Entirely hardy
g Any shape but must be
shallow.

a **Box** (Buxus) **/M/B
b Small shrub with very hard
wood and tiny evergreen leaves.

Very slow growing.
c Collected wildlings; old
unwanted 'dutch garden'
hedges; container-grown;
cuttings.
d Informal upright; slanting;
literati; driftwood; split-trunk;
groups.
e Mk1.
f Entirely hardy
g Rectangular; oval, circular.

a **Camellia, especially
Sasanqua varieties** */M/!
b Half-hardy evergreen shrub
with very large soft petalled
flowers in a variety of colours.
c Container-grown.
d Informal upright; literati;
cascade.
e Mk1 with added leaf mould.
f Protect from strong sunlight
and wind and provide winter
protection.
g Glazed ornamental pots of
hexagonal or circular shape.

a **Cedar** (Cedrus spp)
*****/M/B
b Large coniferous tree with
bright green needles clustered in
rosettes. Also pendulous and
blue varieties.
c Container-grown stock; seed.
d All except broom; twisted
trunk; exposed root and stump
style.
e Mk1 or Mk2.
f Protect roots of freshly potted
trees from frost.
g Rectangular; oval; square;
circular; slabs; crescents.

a **Cherry** (Prunus spp)
*****/M/B
b Small deciduous tree with very
attractive clusters of flowers in
pink, white and cerise in early
spring. Occasionally bears
fruit. The wild variety is the
most coveted.
c Collected wildlings;
container-grown; graftings.
d Informal upright; slanting;
semi-cascade; cascade; literati;
broom; twin-trunk; and
especially split and hollow trunk
with large trees.
e Mk1 or Mk2.
f Full sun. Provide winter
protection.
g Ornamental glazed
rectangular; oval; circular; also
slabs and crescents.

a **Cotoneaster horizontalis**
****/M/B
b Flowering shrub with minute
leaves and bright red berries in
autumn. Trunk usually fairly

thin. Other varieties worth
trying are: Compacta;
Compacta nana; Microphyllus;
Congestus.
c Self-sown seedlings are readily
available in most gardens;
collected wildlings; cuttings;
air-layerings.
d Most, apart from driftwood;
stump. Exceptionally good for
'mame' Bonsai.
e Mk1 or Mk2.
f Entirely hardy. Full sun.
g Glazed pots to compliment
colour of berries. Ovals;
circular and soft-edged.

a **Crab apple** (Malus spp)
*****/M/B/
b There are several suitable
varieties of this deciduous tree to
try for Bonsai eg. Malus
almey; M.eleyi; M.floribunda;
M.golden hornet; M.halliana;
M.kaido; M.x purpurea; M.x
robusta and many others. My
favourite is M.x robusta grafted
onto apple seedling rootstock.
Medium-sized tree that flowers
profusely in spring and
produces attractive miniature
apples in autumn.
c Mostly grafted onto a variety
of rootstocks.
d Any of the single trunked
styles and possibly 'mother and
son'.
e Mk1.
f Entirely hardy. Full sun.
g Decorative glazed pots with
soft edges and medium depth.

a **Cryptomeria japonica** *****
b Large straight trunked
coniferous tree with reddish
shredding bark and short
awl-shaped bright green leaves
resembling the Wellingtonia.
c Container-grown; imported
specimens; cuttings.
d Formal upright; split-trunk;
multiple plantings and forest
groups.
e Mk2.
f Fairly hardy but will benefit
from some winter protection.
g Unglazed reddish formal
rectangular; slabs.

a **Cycad** (Cycas spp) ***/!
b Primitive palm-like foliage
growing from top of rough short
trunk. Very much a curiosity in
Bonsai circles but fun to try.
c Container-grown; imports;
seed.
d Virtually untrainable into any
style. Allow to grow as it
chooses.
e Mk2.

*f* Semi-tropical, therefore requires heated winter protection and prefers a greenhouse in summer.
*g* Deepish rectangular unglazed pot.

*a* **Cypress** (Chamaecyparis spp) \*\*\*\*/M/B
*b* Numerous varieties of cypresses are available. They are coniferous trees varying enormously in size with somewhat frond-like foliage and reddish shredding bark. The genetic dwarf varieties such as Chamaecyparis obtusa nana gracilis are amongst the most popular.
*c* Container-grown grafted specimens; cuttings.
*d* Most, apart from broom.
*e* Mk2.
*f* Most are very hardy but provide some winter protection to be safe.
*g* Reddish unglazed rectangular pots of medium depth; slabs.

*a* **Elm** (Ulmus spp)
A very general name covering many sub-species such as:

*a* **Chinese elm** (Ulmus parvifolia) \*\*\*\*/M/B
*b* Small deciduous tree that retains its tiny green leaves late into December. The species includes rough and smooth bark varieties. Thick spaghetti-like roots.
*c* Imports; air-layerings; cuttings.
*d* Most upright styles especially informal upright and broom; forest groups; avoid exposed root, twisted trunk and clump.
*e* Mk1.
*f* Semi-shade in summer with frost protection in winter.
*g* Rectangular; oval.

*a* **English elm** (Ulmus procera) \*\*\*\*/M/B
*b* A variable deciduous species almost totally wiped out by Dutch elm disease. Leaves relatively small and somewhat rough in texture. There are many other varieties of elm worth considering for Bonsai including the catlin elm and Siberian elm.
*c* Collected suckers; air-layerings; cuttings.
*d* Informal upright; slanting; broom; twin-trunk; clump; forest groups; raft; sinuous.
*e* Mk1.
*f* Entirely hardy. Provide some

shade in summer.
*g* Muted glazed rectangular; square; circular.

*a* **Fig** (Ficus spp) \*/!
*b* Very large leaves. A curiosity tree that is attractive to some people. Some of the dwarf creeping forms of fig such as: Ficus thunbergii and F.pumila are well worth using as under-plantings in conjunction with root-over-rock style Bonsai. They look very much like a dwarf ivy when used in this way.
*c* Container-grown; cuttings.
*d* Informal upright.
*e* Mk1.
*f* Full sun in summer; winter protection from frost.
*g* Deep glazed rugged rectangular and oval.

*a* **Firethorn** (Pyracantha spp) \*\*\*\*/M/B
*b* Very common evergreen shrub that produces clusters of tiny cream flowers in late spring and brilliant yellow, orange or red berries in autumn which look gorgeous against the dark green leaves. Very popular with blackbirds.
*c* Unwanted garden specimen trees and hedges; container-grown; air-layerings; cuttings; seed.
*d* Prime order of five; literati; mother and son; split-trunk.
*e* Mk1.
*f* Although hardy as a garden shrub it is very vulnerable to frost when in a pot so provide winter protection. Also protect berries from birds.
*g* Blue/green glazed oval; rectangular; hexagonal; scalloped; petal shaped.

*a* **Ginkgo** \*\*\*\*\*/M/B/!
*b* Very much a botanical curiosity of interesting ancestry (it has remained unchanged in the evolutionary cycle for over 160 million years). It reproduces itself through a process known as Oogamy which involves a motile sperm that fertilizes the seed after the fruit has fallen. A large upright tree with large glaucus green leathery leaves that look like the maidenhair fern. The yellowish plum-like fruits smell like babies' vomit if crushed.
*c* Container-grown; cuttings; air-layerings; seed.
*d* Upright; clump; cluster.
*e* Mk1.

*f* Fairly hardy but the new leaves are prone to damage from frost. Provide winter protection.
*g* Glazed ornamental oval, rectangular.

*a* **Hawthorn** (Crataegus spp) \*\*\*\*\*/M/B
*b* Medium-sized deciduous flowering tree. Flowers white, pink or red depending on variety. Multi-lobed leaves. Plum red berries in autumn. Easily trained.
*c* Collected wildlings; unwanted garden hedges etc; air-layerings; cuttings; graftings (of cultivars); seed.
*d* Most apart from broom. Best suited for large Bonsai in dramatic driftwood or split-trunk styles.
*e* Mk1.
*f* Entirely hardy. Full sun.
*g* Glazed rectangular; oval; scalloped; petal shaped.

*a* **Hazel** (Corylus spp) \*\*
*b* Large rough-leaved hedgerow shrub. Generally uninteresting.
*c* Collected wildlings; container-grown.
*d* Informal upright; slanting.
*e* Mk1.
*f* Entirely hardy. Full sun.
*g* Rectangular; square; ornamental.

*a* **Hemlock** (Tsuga spp) \*\*\*/M/B
*b* Several varieties. Mostly large coniferous upright trees with short flattish green linear leaves not unlike those of the yew but more delicate in appearance. Some of the dwarf varieties may prove better for Bonsai.
*c* Container-grown; seed.
*d* Most of the upright styles other than broom; twin-trunk; forest groups; split-trunk; mother and son; windswept.
*e* Mk2.
*f* Hardy, full sun.
*g* Shallow formal rectangular pots to enhance height of tree.

*a* **Holly** (Ilex spp) \*\*\*/M/B
*b* Hollies differ considerably as a species. The Christmas type is virtually useless for Bonsai but some of the dwarf varieties (I.crenata, and its variants) are very good. Small tree with smooth silvery white bark and elliptic greeny-grey leaves with purplish veins. Plump red berries. Black berries on some of the dwarf varieties. Must be cross pollinated for fruit to

develop.
*c* Imports; cuttings.
*d* Informal upright mostly.
*e* Prefers acid soils. Mk1 plus additional peat.
*f* Provide some winter protection.
*g* Glazed ornamental to compliment colour of berries; rectangular; oval.

*a* **Honeysuckle** (Lonicera spp) \*\*\*\*/M/B
*b* Lonicera nitida (dwarf variety mostly used for hedges), is probably the most suitable for Bonsai. Flaky buff coloured bark on vine-like trunks; extremely small dark green leaves. Also a golden variety. This species does not enjoy the popularity it deserves.
*c* Hedges; container-grown; cuttings.
*d* Most. Also suitable for 'wrap-arounds'. Generally very versatile.
*e* Mk1.
*f* Very hardy; full sun.
*g* Decorative glazed soft-edged pots to compliment style.

*a* **Hornbeam** (Carpinus spp) \*\*\*\*\*/M/B
*b* The Japanese varieties are softer in leaf texture than the common variety (C.betulus) which is a medium to large deciduous tree with bright green leaves very similar to the beech but more obviously ribbed between the veins. Dark grey-brown bark. Some of the Japanese varieties display spectacular autumn colour.
*c* Collected wildlings; container-grown' imports' cuttings; air-layerings.
*d* All, but especially upright and hollow trunk.
*e* MK1.
*f* Leaves prone to sunburn. Semi-shade in summer with some protection in winter from extreme cold.
*g* Rectangular; oval; circular of medium depth.

*a* **Horse chestnut** (Aesculus spp) \*/!
*b* A large deciduous tree with huge compound palmate green leaves which are really too big for adapting sensibly for Bonsai. However, some people insist on the species and I must confess I have seen one or two quite nice Bonsai from this source. The bark is smooth and characterless and the branches

and twigs very thick and stiff in growth habit. Altogether too much like hard work of the masochistic kind.
c Collected wildlings; seed.
d Best for very large Bonsai, although I do have a twelve-year-old 'Mame' conker of only five inches (13cm) in height. The world is full of contradictions. Upright; informal upright; hollow trunk; groups.
e MK1.
f Entirely hardy.
g Rectangular.

a Ivy (Hedera spp) **/M/B/!
b Very common vine with many variants.
c Unwanted garden plants; cuttings; air-layerings; container-grown.
d Best suited for 'mame' and 'shohin' Bonsai.
e MK1.
f Entirely hardy but likes some protection from strong sun in summer.
g Glazed decorative pots in ornamental shapes.

a Jasmine (Jasminum spp) ****/M
b The winter, yellow flowering variety (J.nudiflorum) is the most popular for Bonsai. Dark green trifoliate leaves which may remain on plant in mild winters. Flowers which appear in late winter are very attractive and bring some cheer into the dark cold months of winter.
c Container-grown; imports; cuttings; air-layering.
d Upright; broom; s.cascade; cascade.
e Mk1.
f Full sun in summer.
g Pale-blue glazed rectangular or oval with some ornamentation.

a Juniper (Juniperus spp) *****/M/B
A very large genus of shrubby trees of which several species are well suited for training into Bonsai. The main groupings are related to the nature of the leaf. That is, awl-shaped (eg. J.rigida; J.communis; J.squamata etc), and scale-like (eg. J.chinensis; J.californica; J.blaauw etc). There are so many varieties that are suitable that you will have to experiment for yourself but I have included below some of the more popular species.

a Common juniper (J. communis)
b Straggly shrub with glaucus blue/green awl-shaped leaves; very prickly. Twisting trunk with rich reddish bark.
c Collected wildlings; cuttings; air-layerings; seed.
d Literati; windswept; informal upright; driftwood; s.cascade; cascade.
e Mk2.
f Full sun.
g Reddish unglazed shallow round; oval.

a Needle juniper (J. rigida)
b Very prickly awl-shaped leaves. Not unlike common juniper but the trunk is stockier and the shoots slightly frond-like. Trunk rugged with numerous branches (very suitable for jinning); bark greyish-brown.
c Imports; cuttings; seed.
d Best species for driftwood style; also informal upright; s.cascade; cascade; forest groups.
e Mk2.
f Full sun in summer; give some protection from frost in winter.
g Chunky rectangular; slabs; crescents.

a J. squamata 'meyeri'
b One of the many dwarf varieties now enjoying popularity as Bonsai. Reddish flaking bark on somewhat stiff trunk and branches. Bluey-green glaucus awl-shape leaves; sharp. Branch tips tend to droop. Often considerable die-back of foliage that has been denied light.
c Container-grown; cuttings; air-layerings.
d Informal upright; literati; s.cascade; cascade; forest groups; twisted trunk.
e Mk2.
f Full sun.
g Rectangular; oval circular; slabs; crescents.

a J. chinensis 'sargentii' (Japanese reference: 'shimpaku')
b Delicious deep green/blue dense scale-like foliage. Trunk tends to twist in growth with rich reddish bark. Often sports natural jins. One of the most popular species for Bonsai in Japan and not without good reason. A must for all Bonsai enthusiasts. Often grafted onto other forms of juniper such as

J.californica to improve foliage and capitalize on the massive trunk of the Californian juniper. Other very similar junipers worth trying are the varieties: Blaauw, Californica, Prostrata and San Jose, to name but a few.
c Imports, cuttings; air-layerings.
d Driftwood; informal upright; s.cascade; cascade. Very suitable for 'wrap-arounds'.
e Mk2.
f Full sun.
g Reddish unglazed rectangular; oval; slabs; crescents.

a Laburnum ****/M/B
b The 'golden rain' tree is a small elegant ornamental with racemes of yellow flowers which later develop into seed pods. (NB. these seeds are very poisonous.)
c Unwanted garden trees; Container-grown; air-layerings; cuttings.
d Upright; slanting; s.cascade; cascade; forest groups.
e Mk1.
f Full sun.
g Ornamental glazed hexagonal; round; oval; petal shape.

a Larch (Larix spp) *****/M/B
b Conifer of straight upright growth. Delicate branches with rosettes of pale green acicular (needle-like) leaves that drop off in autumn. Produces cones at an early age. A very versatile species and possibly the best for beginners to start off with.
c Collected wildlings; container-grown; seed.
d Any style other than broom.
e Mk2.
f Exceptionally hardy; full sun.
g Unglazed rectangular; oval; square; slabs; crescents.

a Lilac (Syringa spp) */M/B
b The only species worth considering is the dwarf variety, S.palibiniana which is a small shrub with ovate to rhomboidal or rounded leaves; dark green. Pale clusters of lilac-pink flowers.
c Container-grown.
d Informal upright; broom.
e Mk1.
f Full sun.
g Glazed ornamental oval; petal-shaped.

a Lime (Tilia spp) **/B
b A large parkland tree with smooth greyish bark and bright pale green leaves. Branches somewhat stiff in growth habit and fairly thick with rounded buds.
c Container-grown; collected wildlings occasionally.
d Upright; broom; groups; hollow and split-trunk.
e Mk1.
f Full sun.
g Rectangular; oval; round.

a Locust (Robinia spp) **/M/B/!
b Medium-sized deciduous tree with light greyish-silver crusty bark. Leaves pinnate and bright green, sometimes yellow. Very attractive to some people. Unfortunately when the leaves are shed the remaining tree looks rather sparse and twig-like.
c Container-grown; from suckers; seed.
d Informal upright.
e Mk1.
f Full sun with winter protection.
g Shallow glazed ornamental oval or round to compliment foliage colour.

a London plane (Platanus spp) **
b Very large deciduous tree with flaking bark and large leaves similar to the sycamore. Stiff in growth habit and somewhat coarse. Better suited for very large Bonsai.
c Container-grown.
d Upright and informal upright.
e Mk1.
f Semi-shade in summer.
g Glazed oval; round.

a Magnolia */!
b Sparsely branched flowering shrub of several varieties. Flowers and leaves usually very large.
c Container-grown.
d Informal upright.
e Mk1.
f Full sun with protection in winter.
g Shallow glazed round; scalloped or petal shape.

a Maple (see Acer)

a Metasequoia ****/B
b Also known as the dawn redwood. A very fast growing coniferous tree that sheds its

frond-like green flattish linear leaves in autumn. Trunk straight with bright reddish fibrous bark.
c Container-grown; cuttings.
d Formal upright; twin-trunk; mother and son; forest groups.
e Mk 1 with plenty of water in summer.
f Semi-shade in summer.
g Large shallow unglazed oval and rectangular.

a **Myrtle** (Myrtus) \*\*/M/B/!
b Attractive flowering shrub with many variants.
c Container-grown; cuttings.
d Informal upright; broom.
e Mk 1.
f Full sun with some protection in winter.
g Shallow glazed ornamental.

a **Nandina** \*\*\*\*/B/!
b The sacred bamboo' as it is also known looks like a cross between a bamboo and berberis. The leaves often turn brilliant colours in autumn.
c Container-grown; division of culms (root stems).
d Mostly used as an accent planting.
e Mk 1.
f Full sun but protected from wind; winter protection required.
g Shallow decorative glazed ovals; crescents; hexagonal.

a **Oak** (Quercus spp) \*\*\*
b Large deciduous hardwood tree with lobed leaves and acorns. Numerous varieties worth investigating, particularly the cork bark species. Somewhat prone to pests and diseases when grown as Bonsai. Very slow growing.
c Collected wildlings; seed.
d Informal upright; slanting; multi-trunk; hollow and split-trunk; octopus; clump; broom.
e Mk 1.
f Protect from full sun and provide protection in winter.
g Rugged rectangular; oval. Fairly deep.

a **Peach** (Prunus spp) \*\*\*/M/B
b Small flowering tree. Usually grafted. Leaves rather large. Prone to peach leaf curl disease.
c Imports; grafting; container-grown.
d Broom; informal upright; hollow trunk.
e Mk 1.

f Full sun.
g Decorative glazed soft-edged pots

a **Persimmon** (Diospyros spp) \*\*\*/!
b Small tropical tree with very large leaves. Large edible orangy-peach coloured fruits.
c Difficult to find; imports; occasionally container-grown.
d Split or hollow trunk.
e Mk 1.
f Greenhouse in summer with heat in winter.
g Glazed ornamental soft-edged.

a **Pine** (Pinus spp) \*\*\*\*\*/M/B
b Without any doubt pines are the aristocrats of Bonsai. Many species of coniferous trees with needle-like leaves in groups of two, three and five. I have listed below some of the most popular varieties but there are many more worth trying.

a **Japanese white pine** (P.parviflora) \*\*\*\*\*/M/B
b Five needle pine with short bluey-green needles that have a slight twist. Bark dark grey. Innumerable cultivars, mostly grafted onto Japanese black pine rootstocks (eg: P.adcock's dwarf; P.zui-sho; P.brevifolia; P.corticosa etc).
c Imports; container-grown; grafting; seed.
d All except broom.
e Mk 2.
f Full sun.
g Unglazed rectangular; oval; slabs.

a **Japanese black pine** (P.thunbergii) \*\*\*\*\*/M/B
b Fairly long straight dark-green robust needles carried in pairs of two per sheath. Medium-size coniferous tree with attractive chunky silvery-black bark. Innumerable cultivars including several of the cork-bark varieties (ie. the corticosa/corticata cultivars). These latter are usually grafted.
c Imports; container-grown; grafting; air-layerings; occasionally from cuttings (difficult); seed.
d All except broom.
e Mk 2.
f Full sun.
g Rugged unglazed rectangular occasionally oval; crescents; slabs.

a **Japanese red pine** (P.densiflora) \*\*\*\*/M/B
b Less popular than the white or black pines. Probably because the twigs are somewhat brittle and therefore difficult to train. Coniferous two-needle pine with pale creamy-green leaves and reddish bark on mature trees.
c Imports; container-grown; air-layering; seed.
d All except broom.
e Mk 2.
f Full sun.
g Shallow unglazed rectangular; oval; slabs.

a **Scots pine** (P.sylvestris) \*\*\*\*\*/M/B
b Possibly the finest species of pine to use for Bonsai. Exceptionally versatile and incredibly hardy. Large elegant tall coniferous tree with reddish-orange bark on mature specimens. Shortish bluey-green needles in pairs of two, occasionally thick. Very variable. Innumerable varieties, mostly grafted genetic dwarfs such as: var.Beuvronensis; Andorra; Frensham; Dansai (my own variety); Watereri; Doone valley; Viridis compacta; Nana; Pygmaea; Nisbet's gem and others. More are being added to the list each year. Scots pines are without any doubt my favourite species of tree for Bonsai.
c Collected wildlings; container-grown; purchased specimens; air-layering; seed.
d Any except broom but especially, literati.
e Mk 2.
f Full sun but most pines improve their colour if given some shade — this is useful if you intend to exhibit your trees.
g Shallow unglazed reddish rectangular; oval; round; slabs; crescent.

**Other pine species**
I have included below the names and star ratings of other pines that are worth using for Bonsai. If five-needle, treat as P.parviflora; if two-needle or three-needle treat as P.sylvestris.

**Mountain pine** (P.mugo) \*\*\*\*/M/B Two-needle.
**Jack pine** (P.banksiana) \*\*\*\*/M/B Two-needle.
**Arolla pine** (P.cembra) \*\*\*/M/B Five-needle.
**Korean pine** (P.koraiensis)

\*\*\*/M/B Five-needle.
**Austrian pine** (P.nigra) \*\*\* Two-needle.
**Western yellow pine** (P.ponderosa) \*\*\*\* Three-needle.
**Siberian pine** (P.pumila) \*\*\*\*/M/B Five-needle.
**Weymouth pine** (P.strobus var.nana) \*\*\*/B Five-needle.

a **Pomegranate** (Punica spp) \*\*\*/M/B/!
b The dwarf variety is best suited for Bonsai. Small shrub with bright green leaves on gingery-chestnut twigs. Flowers and fruits produced freely when kept in a greenhouse.
c Cuttings; seed.
d Ideal for 'mame' or informal upright.
e Mk 1.
f Requires heat — could be used for indoor Bonsai. Give ample light.
g Decorative glazed ornamental pots.

a **Poplar** (Populus spp) \*/!
b Large very fast-growing tree with big leathery leaves. Really a bit too fast growing for Bonsai. The aspen is probably the best variety for Bonsai.
c Cuttings.
d Informal upright; hollow and split-trunk.
e Mk 1 with ample water in summer.
f Full sun.
g Glazed round; rectangular; oval.

a **Potentilla** \*\*\*/M/B
b Small garden shrub with attractive flowers a little like a wild rose. Pretty leaves and bark.
c Container-grown; cuttings; seed.
d Best for 'mame' and 'shohin' Bonsai.
e Mk 1.
f Full sun.
g Decorative glazed ornamental pots.

a **Privet** (Ligustrum spp) \*\*\*/M/B
b Very common shrub used mostly for hedges. Dark green leaves.
c Unwanted hedges.
d Informal upright; hollow and split-trunk.
e Mk 1.
f Full sun.
g Glazed rectangular; oval; round.

a **Quince** (Cydonia and pseudocydonia spp) *****/M/B/!
b The cydonia varieties of quince are medium-sized brightly flowering garden shrubs and have thinnish trunks that are grown mostly against walls and as hedges. The pseudocydonia species is the large thick-trunked tree variety that makes the big round attractive fruits. Both varieties have very pretty flowers but rather large coarse leaves. Both are deciduous.
c Imports; container-grown; air-layerings; cuttings.
d Informal upright; cluster groups; accent plantings (Cydonia spp).
e Mk1.
f Full sun with winter protection for pseudocydonia.
g Decorative glazed ornamental rectangular; oval; deepish.

a **Rhododendron** (Azalea spp) *****/M/B
b The rhododendron genus is vast and the selection of species somewhat confused. The most popular varieties are undoubtedly the Japanese `satsuki' azaleas which offer an unequalled range of flowering shrubs in every shape, size and colour. Unfortunately, there are very few British propagators of this species so one is virtually forced to buy imported trees. There are also other varieties of dwarf rhododendrons worth trying: R.impeditum; R.blue tit.
c Imports, occasionally container-grown; air-layerings, cuttings.
d All.
e Must be free of lime. Mk1 with additional peat.
f Shaded position in summer with winter protection.
g Decorative glazed ornamental deepish rectangular; oval.

a **Ribes** */M/!
b The gooseberries and flowering currants are occasionally used for `shohin' Bonsai as curiosities. Soft garden fruit bush with prickly branches.
c Unwanted garden plants.
d Informal upright `shohin' and `mame'.
e Mk1.
f Full sun.
g Decorative glazed ornamental.

a **Rowan** (Sorbus spp)

*****/M/B
b Also known as the mountain ash. Smallish tree with pinnate leaves and cream-coloured flowers that produce clusters of brilliant orange-red berries in autumn.
c Collected wildlings; seed.
d Informal upright; windswept; split-trunk.
e Mk1.
f Full sun.
g Glazed rectangular; oval; round.

a **Sea buckthorn** (Hippophae spp) **/M/B/!
b Attractive shrub often found by the coast. The silvery-grey-green textured leaves are linear and very slightly curved. Clusters of orange berries. Stems thorny.
c Container-grown; cuttings.
d Best suited to `shohin' and `mame'; informal upright.
e Mk1.
f Full sun.
g Decorative glazed oval; rectangular.

a **Sequoia and Sequoiadendron** ****/B
b Both Californian redwood and Wellingtonia are very similar but their leaves differ significantly. The C.redwood has flattish linear yew-like leaves and the Wellingtonia has awl-shaped scale-like leaves not unlike Cryptomeria japonica. Both are massive coniferous trees with reddish-brown fibrous bark and descending branches. The C.redwood tends to produce many suckers from its base. Both species enjoy plenty of water.
c Container grown, air-layering; cuttings.
d Formal upright; split-trunk; twin-trunk; Forest groups.
e Mk1.
f Semi-shade in summer with winter protection.
g Large shallow rectangular or oval unglazed reddish-brown. Be sure to mound up soil.

a **Spiraea** **/M/B/
b A large genus of flowering shrubs with refined foliage and twigs.
c Container-grown; unwanted garden plants; cuttings.
d Best used for `shohin' and `mame' Bonsai.
e Mk1.
f Full sun with winter protection.

g Decorative glazed ornamental pots; slabs; tufa.

a **Spruce** (Picea spp) *****/M/B
b The classic species amongst the spruces is P.jezoensis. Also popular are: P.hondoensis and P.glehnii but all of these species are difficult to obtain in the UK and need to be imported. There are many readily available dwarf varieties such as: Picea glauca albertiana conica; P.mariana nana; and many others. Large or small coniferous trees with Christmas-tree-like foliage.
c Imports; container-grown; air-layering; cuttings; seed.
d All except broom but especially formal upright and forest groups.
e Mk2.
f Full sun.
g Formal rectangular; shallow oval; slabs; crescents.

a **Stewartia** (monodelpha) ***
b Ornamental shrub with very attractive chestnut-red flaking bark. Leaves colour up beautifully in autumn.
c Imports; container-grown.
d Upright; forest groups.
e Lime-free Mk1 with added peat.
f Semi-shade in summer with winter protection.
g Shallow oval.

a **Sweet chestnut** (Castanea spp) */!
b Massive deciduous tree with very large leaves that do not reduce easily.
c Collected wildlings; container-grown; seed.
d Informal upright; hollow or split-trunk.
e Mk1 with added leaf-mould.
f Full sun.
g Deepish glazed rectangular and oval.

a **Sweet gum** (Liquidambar spp) ***/M/B
b Not unlike the larger maples. Thick large dark-green leaves which turn a spectacular crimson in autumn. Medium to large tree with bark that is sometimes corky.
c Container-grown; air-layerings; cuttings.
d Informal upright; twin trunk.
e Mk1.
f Semi-shade in summer.
g Glazed oval, deepish.

a **Sycamore** (Acer pseudoplatanus spp) *
b A very large commonplace tree that has thick stiff characterless twigs with large leaves that do not reduce easily. Smooth unattractive bark.
c Collected wildlings.
d Informal upright.
e Mk1.
f Full sun.
g Rectangular; oval.

a **Tamarisk** (Tamarix spp) ****/M/B
b A medium-sized tree often grown along seafront promenades. The tiny pink flowers precede the graceful plume-like foliage opening in early spring. Very wind resistant.
c Unwanted garden trees; container-grown; air-layerings; cuttings.
d Windswept; slanting; informal upright; hollow and split-trunk; weeping.
e Mk1.
f Full sun.
g Shallow glazed oval.

a **Taxodium** ****
b The swamp cypress is a tall coniferous tree with reddish-brown fibrous bark and flattened linear leaves that fall off in the autumn. It likes lots of water.
c Container-grown.
d Formal upright; twin-trunk; forest groups; windswept.
e Very damp Mk1 with added peat.
f Semi-shade in summer with protection in winter.
g Large shallow unglazed reddish rectangular; oval.

a **Umbrella pine** (Sciadopitys spp) ***/!
b A curious medium-sized conifer with clustered whorls of flattish dark-green leaves. Exfoliating bark that reveals the reddish-brown new bark underneath. Much more popular in Japan than the UK. Very much an esoteric choice.
c Container-grown.
d Informal upright.
e Mk1.
f Semi-shade in summer.
g Reddish-brown unglazed medium depth rectangular and oval.

a **Willow** (Salis spp) ****/M/B
b The weeping willow is undoubtedly the best known of

this large genus of tree that comes in all shapes and sizes. All like plenty of water.
c Cuttings; container-grown; collected wildlings.
d Usually with weeping branches but sometimes pollarded; informal; s.cascade; cascade. The dwarf varieties can be used for accent and under-plantings as well as 'shohin' and 'mame'.
e Mk1.
f Semi-shade in summer with some winter protection.
g Medium depth glazed round or oval.

a Wisteria *****/B
b Beautiful vine with large

racemes of purple, mauve or white flowers and pinnate leaves.
c Container-grown grafted trees; unwanted garden specimens.
d Usually upright with weeping outspread branches to encourage flowers to 'weep'; s.cascade; cascade; slanting. Could also be used with 'wrap-arounds'.
e Mk1 with plenty of water in summer.
f Full sun in summer with protection in winter.
g Decorative glazed deepish round or oval.

a Yew (Taxus spp) ****/M/B

b Medium-sized coniferous tree with deep-green flattish linear leaves and beautiful ox-blood red bark that tends to form scales. Often found in churchyards where they are said to cast off the 'evil-eye'.
c Collected wildlings; container-grown; air-layerings.
d Formal uprights; informal upright; s.cascade; driftwood; slanting. Avoid broom.
e Mk2.
f Roots very susceptible to frost damage so provide winter protection; semi-shade in summer.
g Rectangular; oval; slabs.

a Zelkova ****/M/B

b The Japanese grey-bark elm is one of the best deciduous species of tree for Bonsai. A large tree with beautiful smooth silver-grey bark covered in tiny reddish-orange lenticels (pores). Very small elliptic leaves on exceptionally refined twigs. Also worth trying is the caucasian elm: Z.carpinifolia.
c Imports; air-layering; container-grown; cuttings; seed.
d The classic species for growing in the broom style; informal upright.
e Mk1.
f Full sun with some protection in winter.
g Shallow glazed round; oval; rectangular.

# Glossary

**Abscission** The shedding of leaves.

**Adventitious** (of buds) Buds that develop sporadically in unusual parts of the tree.

**Air-layer** Horticultural technique used to promote roots to form on a branch above soil level.

**Apex** The culminating or highest point of the Bonsai.

**Apical** (of buds) The end or terminal bud on a branch or apex of a tree's trunk.

**Arbrex*** Black wound sealant used to protect pruned roots and branches etc. Available from most garden centres in the UK and some other countries.

**Auxins** Any of several plant hormones that promote cell elongation.

**Bonsai** Japanese word translated, literally meaning 'tree in a tray'.

**Cambium** Green layer of single cells between the bark and the sapwood of trees and most plants.

**Compost** Medium in which Bonsai or other plants are grown.

**Cuprinol*** Trade name for a chemical compound used as a wood preservative. Very toxic — use with care! Manufactured by: Cuprinol Ltd, Adderwell, Frome, Somerset, BA11 1NL, UK.

**Dormancy** Period when the plant is resting and growth is inactive — usually from late autumn to early spring.

**En Mag*** A no-lime release fertilizer developed mostly for use with rhododendrons, azaleas and ericacious species and marketed by: Chempak Products, Bingley Road, Hoddesdon, Herts, EN11 0LR, UK.

**Friable** Readily crumbled; with reference to soil.

**Hortag*** Fired clay balls normally used for capillary beds as a base on which to stand potted plants to improve humidity and also to allow water intake from the soil.

**Internode** Portion of plant stem that forms between sets of buds.

**Jin** The Japanese name for a dead bleached branch that has had its bark removed.

**Kyonal*** A Japanese product used to seal and protect from infection the cut ends of pruned roots and branches etc. Available from most Bonsai nurseries.

**Mame** The Japanese name for 'bean-size' Bonsai; usually never more than six inches (15 cms) in any direction inclusive of pot.

**Mycelium** The vegetative part of a fungus consisting of a mass of branching threadlike filaments called hyphae.

**Mycorrhiza** The symbiotic association of the mycelium of a fungus with the roots of certain plants, especially conifers.

**Osmocote*** A highly concentrated fertilizer encapsulated in resin and marketed in the UK by: Chempak Products, Bingley Road, Hoddesdon, Herts, EN11 0LR, UK.

**Osmosis** Of the soil — a chemical imbalance, usually caused by excessive fertilizing, which results in the inability of the plant to take up water and often results in its death.

**Perlag*** A pumice-like compound manufactured by: Silvaperl Products Ltd, Harrogate, Yorkshire, UK.

**Ph** The symbol used to indicate the alkalinity/ acidity levels of the soil.

**Phostrogen*** A general purpose fertilizer manufactured by: Phostrogen Ltd, Corwen, Clwyd, Wales, LL21 0EE, UK.

**Photosynthesis** The process by which chlorophyll-containing cells in green plants convert incident light to compounds, especially carbohydrates from carbon dioxide and water, with the simultaneous release of oxygen.

**Potensai** Material stock plant serving as a potential Bonsai. Bonsai undergoing training.

**Radial** (of roots) Roots emerging from many

points around the base of the trunk of a tree rather like the spokes of a bicycle-wheel.

**Ring-barking** The removal of a band of bark (which can vary in width) from all around the trunk of a tree or branch when air-layering or when trying to encourage new roots to form.

**Rootstock** The plant material supplying the roots on to which the scion is to be grafted.

**Scion** The variety of plant that is to be grafted on to a rootstock.

**Sequestrene*** A tonic that helps plants to take up nutrients from the soil when unfavourable Ph levels in the soil would otherwise have an inhibiting effect locking

the natural processes. Manufactured by: Murphy Chemical Ltd, Wheathamstead, St Albans, Herts. AL4 8QU, UK. Flowers of sulphur can be used for the same purpose.

**Shari** The Japanese name for a bleached portion of trunk that has had its bark removed.

**Shohin** The Japanese name for Bonsai that are small but larger than mame Bonsai.

**Stratify** (of seeds) The process of laying seeds in autumn under peat or a similar compound in order to expose them to freezing and thawing conditions to facilitate germination in the spring. This process can also be executed in a refrigerator.

**Suiban** The Japanese name for a shallow container without any drainage holes for displaying *suiseki* in.

**Suiseki** The Japanese name for 'viewing stones' that suggest scenic views such as waterfalls, mountains, islands etc.

**Superthrive*** A chemical compound made up mostly from a wide range of vitamins and hormones and especially useful in helping newly transplanted plants to regenerate their damaged roots. Manufactured by: Vitamin Institute, 5409-15 Satsuma Avenue, No. Hollywood, Cal. USA. Available in the UK from most Bonsai nurseries.

**Turgidity** Of plants — expanded by water intake, increasing brittleness in

the plants' cellular structure.

**Viable** (of seeds) Capable of germinating under favourable conditions.

**Witch's broom** A tightly congested, localized foliage growth found in many species of tree, usually caused by a virus disease.

\* Tradenames for fertilizers, pesticides etc available in the UK and some other countries. If you are unfamiliar with these products or unable to obtain them in your country refer to your local Bonsai society or garden centre, explain the problem and ask whether an equivalent product is available.

# Index

▼ Thistles in the sunset